IT'S TIME TO DO LAW DIFFERENTLY

HOW TO RESHAPE YOUR FIRM AND REGAIN YOUR LIFE

LUCY DICKENS

'*It's Time to Do Law Differently* is a timely and practical handbook for leaders of smaller law firms of all kinds.

'Timely. The tsunami of change for traditional firms is accelerating as a result of the pandemic. If ever there was a time to adapt and transform a law firm's business model, it's now. While there is a growing number of resources to guide larger law firms, there are few for smaller firms which have particular challenges.

'Practical. Smaller law firm leaders by and large know they have to change the way they operate, what they need is the "how to". Lucy Dickens' six-step transformation process shows the way in plain language.'

Dr George Beaton, Co-author of *Remaking Law Firms: Why and How*

'Lucy Dickens has put together a real treat for small law firms – a book that's comprehensive, yet easy to read and digest! Based on excellent experience and knowledge, *It's Time to Do Law Differently* sets out a well thought-out 6-step guide to an optimised legal practice – not just to make more money and achieve greater efficiency, but to give lawyers more time for the things in life that they hold dear. It should be given to every small firm lawyer – and law graduate. During my read of it I kept thinking, Damn, I wish I wrote that!'

Mitchell Kowalski, Author of *The Great Legal Reformation: Notes from the Field* and *Avoiding Extinction: Reimagining Legal Services for the 21st Century*

'If you are a lawyer who is risk averse, loves working in Biglaw/Oldlaw, wants to look the same as your colleagues and competitors, loves filling out timesheets and being measured and rewarded for inputs and time spent, then this is definitely *not* the book for you. If however you are a lawyer who seeks a greater purpose in your professional life, is entrepreneurial, prepared to take some risks, seeks to be different and genuinely cares about your clients and the future of your profession then this is the book for you. You will not be disappointed.'

John Chisholm, Leading Australian legal commentator, Recovering Lawyer and Founder, John Chisholm Consulting

'*It's Time to Do Law Differently* is the perfect guide for law practice owners who are looking to build a firm for the future that combines their technical skill and talent with business smarts. Lucy's simple framework will help you to make shifts in how you practise law and in turn will have you reconnecting with the passion that enticed you to start your firm in the first place.'

Clarissa Rayward, CEO, Brisbane Family Law Centre and Happy Lawyer, Happy Life

'Lucy Dickens is a big influence in the push and momentum to help legal firms evolve new ways of doing business that focus on so much more than just creating revenue. Her approach is smart, structured and inspirational – and those law firms that embrace her message will never look back.'

Andrew Griffiths, International bestselling author, global speaker, The Entrepreneurial Futurist

'This book is going to be THE go to user friendly guide for small law firms (but really all law firms) looking to make a permanent and sustained change to contemporary legal practice. The book, together with Lucy's podcast, will not only provide a "how to" compendium on doing law differently, but might just set you on the path to a more fulfilling life too – you'll want to read this one!'

Terri Mottershead, Executive Director, Centre for Legal Innovation at The College of Law

'Of the many talents of Lucy Dickens, one shines above the others – an ability, not only to understand complex matters, but to communicate them clearly and simply. Such a gift is on full display in this book, generously packed with practical wisdom. Law firm leaders will return here again and again for guidance, and inspiration.'

Michael Hodgkins, Director, Birman & Ride

'Lucy is all about the "how?" and I love that. In a space where there's so much talk about the "what" and the "why", Lucy's approach is refreshing in its pragmatism and focus on action. Her Doing Law Differently podcast elevates the do-ers and experimenters of legal innovation and champions those who are creating enduring change – one step at a time. Lucy is a tireless and committed advocate for thinking differently about what we do every day.'

Katherine Thomas, CEO, Free Range Lawyers

'I've had the privilege of calling Lucy my friend for years now and have personally benefited from many a conversation about running a law firm. She's my go-to person. Now Lucy can be everyone's go-to person with this incredible book, where she generously shares her easy-to-follow framework so you can be a lawyer and still have the lifestyle you want.'

Jo Alilovic, Director, 3D HR Legal

'Through her podcast and her coaching business, Lucy is bringing important topics to light, including new trends in NewLaw, how to be innovative in the legal industry and ways to thrive in the new environment. Lucy is wise beyond her years and embodies the passion for bringing about positive change in the industry. Her reach through her podcast, practice and coaching is broad and will undoubtedly have an impact for years to come.'

Nicole N. Auerbach, Founder Valorem Law Group and ElevateNexLaw

'Honest. Practical. Creative. Lucy provides a refreshingly candid approach to legal services. She has clear thoughts on what law firms can do to improve in the 2020s, and simple steps that firms can take to manage and adjust to those (significant!) changes. She genuinely cares about lawyers and their clients.'

Michael Morrisey, Managing Director, Morrisey Law

'Lucy's coaching has been a gamechanger for me and my business. Not only is her experience and insight invaluable but her personalised approach is refreshing. She doesn't try to make me or my business fit a rigid mould. Rather, she looks at the bigger picture and provides practical guidance on how I can achieve my personal goals for business, law and life. She helps turn business ideas into reality.'

Nikolina Palasrinne, Founder and Principal, Rubix Legal

'Lucy carefully crafts her messaging so as to best engage her audience and leave them not just knowing but also understanding how to "do law differently".'

Ann-Maree David, Executive Director, Queensland College of Law

'Lucy uses her deep curiosity in her quest to do law differently and she brings an abundance of energy to share what she finds with the profession. Change is what we need and Lucy's contributions help us to understand where that change is needed and, more importantly, to visualise what it will look like.'

Melissa Lyon, Associate Principal, Hive Legal

About the author

Like most lawyers, Lucy's career in law started the traditional way: as a law clerk. She quickly discovered that her skills and passion lay not just in the practice of law, but in the business of law too. From early on in her career, she developed her skills in various roles including lawyer, service designer, team leader, HR manager, business analyst, practice manager and marketing manager.

Today, she is known as a leader in legal innovation. While so many people focus on the 'what' and the 'why', Lucy's approach focuses on action. She is all about the 'how', and is just as interested in coming up with ideas as she is seeing them brought to life.

Lucy is a Senior Associate at Birman & Ride, the same law firm where she started her career. She brings together people, process and technology to reshape the provision of legal services, constantly challenging the way things are done to see if they can be improved. Her high standards, ability to lead and inspire others, and facility with technology have been instrumental in the firm bringing new and innovative legal services to the market.

Lucy regularly speaks in professional circles on reinventing legal practice and transforming the profession and is an Adjunct Lecturer at the College of Law. She also works with leaders of small law firms to help them design, package and systemise the delivery of their services so they can eliminate the grunt work and spend more time on the things they love.

Lucy is incredibly self-motivated and constantly pushes herself to do and achieve more. In 2019 she launched her Top 10 podcast, Doing Law Differently, where she explores how the world's most innovative law firms are transforming the legal profession.

She is also the co-host of the successful podcast The Juggle, where she explores topics to career women have a satisfying career and a fulfilling family life.

Lucy holds a Bachelor of Law (Hons) and Bachelor of Arts (Communications) from the University of Western Australia, and a Certificate in Human Centred Service Design from IDEO University.

Lucy lives in Perth, Western Australia with her high school sweetheart, now husband, Jack and their two young children, Lilly and Harry. As much as she loves legal innovation, motherhood is her greatest passion.

lucy@lucydickens.com.au
www.lucydickens.com.au
www.linkedin.com/in/lucy-dickens

Acknowledgements

My name might be on the cover of this book, but like all good things in life, it is the result of a lot of effort by a lot of people.

Jack, thank you for all the times you reschedule your work diary and take the kids so I can record an interview or write some words. Thank you for getting up in the dead of night to train so that I can do my thing in the daylight hours. You are my biggest supporter and my best critic.

My children Lilly and Harry, who are the source of my motivation for all things in life. And, yes Lilly, you can write a book one day too.

Mum, for always helping with the kids. We couldn't do it without you.

Michael Hodgkins, who is so much more than my boss. Thank you for being such a great mentor and friend, for supporting me through all the ups and downs of work and life and for always being on my team. I've said many times that the reason I love my job is because I get to work with you, and that's true.

Jo Alilovic, who has been my sounding board for this book and all things Doing Law Differently from day one. Thank you for the many, many hours of conversation, for always giving honest and complete attention to my questions and never fobbing me off, even when I'm asking you to look at the hundredth icon for the day. Who'd have known that our chance meeting at the Women Lawyers working group would lead to such a great friendship.

Clarissa Rayward, for planting the idea for this book in my head two years ago, for the many late-night chats to help me through crises of confidence and for teaching me about the different shades of peach.

Andrew Griffiths, for all your guidance and mentorship and especially for helping me through the great icon crisis of 2020.

Project management and text design by Michael Hanrahan Publishing
Cover design by Peter Reardon
Author photo by Jason Malouin, Portrait Store

Disclaimer:

Contents

Are you stuck in the trenches every day? 1

Part I: It's time for law firms to change 7

Are you building a business or working a job? 11

Law is now a buyer's market 19

The journey to Productise and Profit 25

Part II: How to implement Productise and Profit in your firm 39

Step 1: Find your vision 43

Step 2: Deeply understand your clients 53

Step 3: Create amazing solutions 69

Step 4: Productise your services 83

Step 5: Embrace modern marketing 121

Step 6: Optimise your operations 139

Productise and Profit 165

Ready, set, action. It's up to you to make it happen. 169

Where to from here? 181

Are you stuck in the trenches every day?

This book is for leaders of small law firms who want to fundamentally change the way they do business. You aren't chasing world domination, you simply want a successful business that brings you joy and meaning, but one that doesn't demand every one of your waking hours. There are other things that are important in life too.

In this book, I share a six-step process that will take you from the burden of traditional law to a product ecosystem that is designed to serve your lifestyle. To get there, you need to let go of traditional notions of what law should look like and open the world of possibilities that come when you ditch the billable-hour business model and redesign your way of working to suit your life.

You can reshape your firm and regain your life.

STUCK IN THE TRENCHES

Does this sound like you?

You started your law firm to escape the daily grind, to have more control over the work you do and to fit your work around your family and other commitments. Maybe you wanted to make a difference in your community and earn a decent living at the same time.

Instead, you're drowning in legal work with barely any time left for your family, let alone anything else. You persist only in the hope that one day, things will be different. Somehow. One day, you'll have hired and trained a junior lawyer who will share some of the load. Who won't leave just as they actually start to generate a profit, and who won't cause management headaches every other week.

Somehow.

All you really want is to take a holiday, or to have more time with your family. To have a short break away from the office to refresh and recharge and find some of that freedom you were chasing when you started your firm in the first place. And to feel less overwhelmed.

Instead, you find yourself stuck in the trenches every day. You're settling documents, writing cheques, supervising staff, answering phones, and after all that rigamarole, you still find yourself tied to your inbox. If you take your foot off the pedal, the whole business slows down.

On top of all this, you're bombarded with messages telling you to innovate, disrupt, automate, and scale your law firm. These constant, often conflicting, messages can be overwhelming, especially if it's not 'more' you're chasing. Haven't you got enough on your plate already?

You've heard about new business models and fixed pricing, but you're too busy doing client work so you can pay the bills that you don't have time to even think about what you should change, let alone how to do it. At the same time, you know that the legal market is changing rapidly, and if you don't catch up soon your business could be left behind.

CHANGING THE WAY YOU DO LAW

The good news is that there is a better way. A way where you pro-actively take control of your business and fundamentally change the way you 'do law'. A way where you can design a profitable business around your purpose and do the work you love. A way that will make it easier for you to switch off and fall asleep at night and that will free up your time to spend with your family, friends and whatever else it is that's important to you.

This isn't about making your business run without you. You might tell me that's what you want, and many people do, but I don't believe you. I don't believe you because, first, there's no such thing, and second, you started your law firm because you want to run it. You're driven by your purpose and passion and crave the self-determination that comes from running your own law firm. You don't want to sit around doing nothing. Instead, what you want, and what this book will help you to achieve, is to run your business instead of letting it run you.

Law school might teach us to be great lawyers, but it doesn't teach us how to be great businesspeople, and in the modern legal market, being a great businessperson is essential to your success.

That's why I'm going to teach you to Productise and Profit.

SO WHO AM I AND WHY SHOULD YOU LISTEN TO ME?

I started my legal career in 2010 as a law clerk at Birman & Ride, a progressive, boutique law firm in Western Australia, and the same firm I still work for today. Just as the job ad promised, I quickly discovered that the role wasn't for the faint-hearted. From day one, I was thrown in at the deep end with real clients, real files and real legal issues.

My practice area was real estate conveyancing. The work was fast paced, high pressure, and I felt like I was always working to someone else's timeline. Back then e-conveyancing was a distant dream. One typo on an original document, a slightly mismatched signature or running five minutes late with an original document would call off a settlement and ruin a client's grand plans of moving into their new home.

I'd often wake in the middle of the night in a panic that I'd forgotten to adjust a special levy, lodge a contract for duties assessment or request trust money on time. What made it worse was that the work was routine. I was doing the same thing over and over, but still feeling stressed. As soon as one file was settled it was straight on to the next, and the worry would start all over again.

Instead of throwing in the towel, I set about improving the system. Working side by side with our firm's technology partner, I developed systems that enabled us to dramatically reduce costs and improve service quality. My mantra became, 'what can I change so I never have to do this again?' We built clever templates that meant we could completely eliminate any double entry of data, designed processes to systemise and simplify the work, and made the software responsible for remembering all those things that would keep me awake at night. Leveraging these benefits and our new flat-rate pricing model, the firm brought revolutionary change to the conveyancing industry in Western Australia.

And that was just the beginning. Taking the lessons, successes and failures from Flat Rate Settlements, we worked through the firm's practice areas one by one, redeveloping our legal services and bringing together people, technology and processes to design and deliver innovative legal services. As we reshaped the business, my role became a mix of lawyer, team leader, HR manager, business analyst, salesperson, marketing manager and service designer. I discovered my skills in business development, and was fortunate enough to be encouraged to foster those skills.

More importantly, we created a business that enables us all to work to our strengths, doing work we love, with people we like, making a decent income and still getting home in time for dinner with the kids.

In 2019 I launched my successful podcast, Doing Law Differently, a weekly show on which I interview forward-thinking law firm leaders to learn about the behind-the-scenes of how they do law differently. I recognised that there's plenty of advice about *why* we need to change the legal industry, but much less about *how* to do it. The podcast was my effort to fill that gap. In many ways, this book is an extension of that.

In writing this book, I draw on my own experience working for a progressive law firm that constantly pushes the boundaries of legal service delivery, as well as my experience having worked with, interviewed, presented to and read about many of the world's leading law firms. I tie together the threads in a practical guide that you can use to design, package and systemise the delivery of your services so you, too, can reshape your law firm and regain your life in the way we have done in our firm.

My stories

Throughout this book I share many stories and examples from Birman & Ride, the law firm where I've spent over a decade experimenting with and implementing ways to do law differently. I tell many of these stories using the collective 'we', as an acknowledgement that the best innovations have come about as a result of a collaborative process. Success – as it so often is – has been a team effort.

HOW TO GET THE MOST OUT OF THIS BOOK

In this book, I share my six-step process that will help you revolutionise your law firm. I call this Productise and Profit.

Each step in the process builds on the one that came before, so you'll get the most out of this book by reading it in order. I suggest you read it completely first so you have a good idea of where you're heading. You can then go back through each step as you start to implement the ideas in your own firm.

The last part of the book is dedicated to giving you practical skills to help you overcome some of the most common objections to implementing change: 'I don't know where to start' and 'I don't have time'.

Of the many law firm leaders I speak to, there's certainly no shortage of great ideas. I've heard plenty of 'I could' and far fewer 'I have'. As you read this book, I want you to keep this in mind. You can have the best ideas in the world, but unless you act on them, nothing will change. You and the others in your firm have a lot to gain by changing the rules of the game. Let that be your motivator.

PART I

It's time for law firms to change

'What has been lost on many in the legal profession is that the ability to deliver legal services is not a right, it's a privilege – one that lawyers must earn every day. If lawyers do not earn that privilege, clients will turn to other service providers.'

Mitchell Kowalski, *Avoiding Extinction: Reimagining legal services for the 21st century*

IN HIS 2012 BOOK *Avoiding Extinction: Reimagining legal services for the 21st century*, Mitchell Kowalski said that the legal profession was 'now entering the most inventive and disruptive period of change that it has ever experienced'. Close to a decade on, we're slowly moving closer to the tipping point of that change. The simple truth is that the market for legal services has changed, and it continues to do so rapidly, so law firms have no choice but to reshape and rethink the way they do business.

Most thought leadership about innovation in the legal profession focuses on the technological, social and market forces that drive law firms to change the way they do business. The piece of the puzzle that is often missing is a conversation about a move to a more sustainable business model, where you build the business you want and deserve, not the business you think others expect you to build or that has been forced on you by circumstances.

Productise and Profit is about building a law firm that will not only survive the changing legal landscape but that will also allow you and your team to regain your lives. And the time to do this is now. The pace of change in law and business in general is growing more rapid every day. As I write this the world is still in the grips of the COVID-19 pandemic, further driving the need for businesses to innovate. Those that don't will be left behind to struggle and fail.

I set the scene of this change by explaining the first lesson: you need to stop thinking of your law firm as a *practice* and start thinking of it as a *business that sells legal products*. I also recap some of the major influences on law firm businesses that mean lawyers are no longer calling the shots, and examine what this means for you. Lastly, I paint a picture of what the journey ahead might look like as you implement Productise and Profit and take your business from a traditional practice to a product ecosystem.

Being an expert at the practice of law does not make you an expert at running a business. This is the heart of the change that lies ahead.

Are you building a business or working a job?

'If your business depends on you, you don't own a business – you have a job. And it's the worst job in the world because you're working for a lunatic!'

Michael E. Gerber, *The E-Myth Revisited*

I was recently coaching a law firm owner. Let's call him Mark. He was crystal clear on his vision to build his business so he could sell it, exit, and go and do something else. He had a clear plan laid out that told him when to hire each new staff member and how quickly he'd go from zero to ten employees.

Mark knew he needed to hire staff to bring his vision to life, but last time he tried that things didn't go so well. He didn't want to let go of the work, fearful that his new employee might not live up to his standards, and he was also lacking the skills to delegate, manage and train. Midway through our conversation, the penny dropped: 'I'm basically an employed lawyer. I may as well get a job and draw a salary. I'm too busy doing legal work to do development.'

Another, who'd been in business for 21 years, confessed to me: 'I need to learn how to run a business – I'm still not 100% sure that I'm doing it right.'

Most lawyers start a law firm after a number of years in employed practice. They dutifully work their way up the career ladder, and as they climb each rung, the resentment slowly builds. They resent the fact that they spend hours chained to a desk, only to take home a small proportion of the revenue they generate. They resent the lack of autonomy they have over the way they practice law. They resent the slow progress to partnership, or being given the crappy clients, or that they're always under pressure to bill more. By the time they take the plunge and start their own law firm, they're experts at what they do, having well and truly honed their craft before they set out in business on their own.

They're experts at the practice of law, but are they experts at business? What most lack are the management and entrepreneurial skills that are essential to business success.

Where they go wrong is that they work *in* the business and not *on* it, and in doing so they create themselves a job. Unlike an employee, though, this job is much more demanding. As well as doing the client work, they have the responsibility for paying the bills, carrying the professional risk and taking care of all the administrative work that comes hand in hand with business: bookkeeping, accounting, filing and recordkeeping, managing staff, cashflow and budgeting, marketing and promotion – the list goes on. On top of that, there's no sick or annual leave – no work means no income. They end up working long hours just to fit it all in and to make sure the lights stay on.

Over 30 years ago, Michael E. Gerber made famous the idea of working *on* your business instead of working *in* your business in his bestselling book, *The E-Myth: Why most businesses don't work and what to do about it*. *The E-Myth* is just as relevant today as it was when Gerber wrote it.

The E-Myth (the entrepreneurial myth) is the mistaken belief that most businesses are started by people with business skills, when in fact most are started by 'technicians' who know nothing about running a business. According to Gerber, to run a successful business, business owners need to balance three personalities:

- the technician

- the manager

- the entrepreneur.

In the legal world, the *technician* is the legal practitioner whose job it is to 'do the work' – give legal advice and show up in court. In other words, the practice of law. The *manager* focuses on achieving results through managing the technicians. The *entrepreneur* works on the business's vision and focuses on closing the gap between where they are today and where they want to be. The technician and manager work *in* the business, while the entrepreneur works *on* it.

A successful business requires all three roles to be dutifully fulfilled.

At the heart of the change that lies ahead is this: you need to start thinking about your firm as a business. The only way to remove yourself as the bottleneck, eliminate the dependency on you and regain your time and freedom is to embrace the role of business owner over and above that of legal practitioner.

The trap that most law firm owners fall into is that they think they're building a business when, in fact, they're creating a job.

A LEGAL PRACTICE OR A BUSINESS THAT SELLS LEGAL SERVICES?

For all the recent hype about legal innovation, I believe that success comes down to simply approaching what we do with some business savvy. The 'future of law' is really about law firms becoming more like other businesses.

To build a successful business that lets you also have a life, you need to stop being the technician and start being the entrepreneur. To do that, you need to shift your mindset from one that focuses on the practice of law to one that focuses on how the business must work.

Consider the distinction between a legal practice and a business that sells legal products, shown in the following table.

A legal practice versus a business that sells legal products

A legal practice	A business that sells legal products
Based around expert legal practitioner	Based around systems
Has no value outside owner	Has value outside owner
Personal brands of individual rainmakers	Business brand and modern marketing
Clients engage individual lawyers	Clients engage the business
Manual labour	Technology enabled
Sells time	Sells solutions
Can't be sold	Can be sold

A legal practice is based on the expertise of its principal. There might be other people supporting her, but she is the one with the legal skills and who provides the services. Clients engage the firm because of her reputation, so without her, the practice isn't worth anything. In time she might hire other staff to help her, perhaps a receptionist to take bookings or a law clerk to carry out research tasks, but these people are there to help her do her job, not to do it for her. She might also hire other lawyers to provide legal services. In this case, she'll leverage their time to make more money, and each lawyer essentially becomes a practice themselves.

A business that sells legal services is different. For a start, it can operate separately from its owner and leverages something other than its owner to make money, be it a business brand, technology, modern marketing, or a combination. To become a true business, the principal needs to shift her focus from *doing the work* to *how the work gets done*. She needs to build a business that can operate independently of her. She needs to extract her intellectual property and build systems around it so it operates like a turnkey franchise. This will allow other staff to operate effectively in the business, even when its owner isn't around, and it also gives her the ability to sell.

Instead of being a collection of people who sell time to produce an income, a business that sells legal services sees the business as producing outside results for the client. It focuses on continuous improvement and on designing effective systems that are reliable, repeatable and deliver a consistent profit.

As Jordan Furlong, author of *Law is a Buyer's Market*, puts it:

> *In the end you need to ask yourself:* 'Is our law firm a platform for lawyers to sell their services? Or is it a business that delivers value to buyers of legal services?'

It's only by building a business that you can free yourself from the constant demands of a practice.

IT'S TIME TO GET TO WORK ON YOUR BUSINESS

When you're managing client files, you're working as a technician. You're answering the phone, meeting clients, writing advice and appearing in court, and while you're doing this, what you're *not* doing is working on your business. Setting it up for success and building the machine that will operate sufficiently so that you can take a holiday.

As Gerber puts it:

> ... *while you're doing it, doing it, doing it, there's something much more important that isn't getting done. And it's the work you're not doing, the strategic work, the entrepreneurial work, that will lead your business forward, that will give you the life you've not yet known.*

Mark, the lawyer I coached who realised he'd created himself a job, made a commitment during our call to embrace the entrepreneurial mindset. He acknowledged that to achieve his goals, he'd need much more than a strategic business plan. Instead, he needed to fundamentally change the way he operated. We spoke about many of the strategies in this book as he set to work on his business. Now armed with the skills he needs to become not only a manager but an entrepreneur, he has since hired his first employee as part of his plan and is on the path to creating a legal business he can sell.

KEY POINTS IN THIS CHAPTER

1. Most businesses are started by lawyers who, although technically highly skilled, lack the entrepreneurial and management skills necessary to run a successful business.

2. To regain control and build a successful business that lets you have time for the other priorities in life, you need to work *on* your business, not just *in* it.

3. A practice is built around and can't be separated from its founder. On the other hand, a business is built around systems that deliver a result for a client.

Law is now a buyer's market

'A traditional law firm exists to provide buyers with access to solutions for their law-related challenges through the application of a lawyer's time and effort. The future law firm will answer to the same description, minus the last nine words.'

Jordan Furlong, *Law is a Buyer's Market: Building a client-first law firm*

THE RAPIDLY EVOLVING PLAYING FIELD

Before we take a deep dive into transforming your law firm, it's helpful to take a look at the playing field.

Scroll through your LinkedIn feed or any legal news website and you'll be greeted with dozens of articles about the future of law, new technology and innovation. Sure, some of this might be hype, but there's no denying that the legal profession is changing and it's important for you to understand why and how. If you're going to embrace the business of running a law firm, you need to have an understanding of the market you're playing in.

Plenty has been written about the changing state of the legal industry, and I don't intend to add to it or to recap it all. Instead, the aim of this chapter is to set the scene to help you understand some of the bigger picture influences on law firm businesses.

Until recently, lawyers have dictated where, when, how, by whom, and for how much our work was carried out. Having enjoyed a monopoly on legal expertise for so long, we've become used to calling the shots and have become immune to many of the ordinary forces of business. Or so we thought.

The legal profession has been built on the assumption of scarcity: scarcity of information, scarce distribution of resources and scarce choice. The power was firmly in lawyers' hands – we were a necessary evil. This gave rise to a myth of legal exceptionalism. No one could quite be sure exactly what we did in those six-minute billable units, but whatever it was, it was special, no one else could offer it, and so clients would have to take it or leave it.

Today, things are different. Information, resources and choice are abundant. Lawyers are no longer calling the shots. Or, to borrow the title of Jordan Furlong's excellent book on the topic, *Law is a Buyer's Market*.

We're deep in the Information Age where, thanks to advances in technology, most people can access information quickly, easily and at low cost. Anyone with an internet connection can now read legislation and reported court cases online, access legal courses and university lectures, read blog posts and legal articles, and watch videos and listen to podcasts by experts sharing their knowledge with the world. Even the most time-poor client will spend 20 minutes Googling their problem before they pick up the phone to call you.

Think about the types of questions that potential clients ask you when they first call. How does that compare to the questions they'd ask even as little as five years ago? I've seen a big shift. Just a few years ago most of the questions were along the lines of, 'My mum has died. What do I need to do with her will?' Today, the most common question is: 'My mum has died. I need a grant of probate. How can you help?' Or, more likely, 'What do you charge and how long will it take?'

A couple of years ago, clients would expect to have to make an appointment with a lawyer in order to be told what legal services could help them with their problem. Today, clients expect that information to be free, given over the phone instantly, or, better yet, available on demand on a website. Clients don't want to pay you to understand their problem and work out what they need, they just care about the outcome.

I recently took a call from a potential client who was tasked with administering a complex estate. After about 15 minutes on the phone I'd worked out exactly what services he needed and how I could help. I talked him through all the things he needed to do and followed up with a written quote. He was impressed. I wasn't the first law firm he'd called, but I was the first business where he'd been able to speak to a lawyer who understood his legal issues. The other firms wanted him to show up to their office for that privilege – and to pay for that in six-minute increments. That approach just won't cut it today. Had I imposed that barrier, I expect the client would have moved on until he found someone willing to tell him what he wanted to hear. And really, who'd blame him? At this point he just wanted to know what to do next and what it would cost him. It was basic information, not complex legal analysis. If you're wondering, yes, we won the business. And, yes, I know it's not always that simple and there are many situations where a deeper understanding of the matter must precede any quote for services; but that too is a service that must be offered persuasively without barriers.

Of course, technology's role in changing the legal profession goes far deeper than access to information. According to the Macquarie Bank *2020 Legal Services Industry Pulse Check*, 83% of firms are using technology to optimise client interactions and 78% of firms are using technology to deliver services more efficiently.

Today, clients can access legal services at the touch of a button, quite literally. Online tools automate the creation of basic legal agreements, custom-designed wizards or 'bots' ask a series of questions to help laypeople work out if they have a legal claim, and even entire court hearings can be carried out over the internet.

I've seen firsthand how technology can be used to make law better, having designed many technological innovations that have transformed the way we provide legal services, some examples of which I'll share with you throughout this book. Our custom-built practice management software, ContactsLaw, has undoubtedly been an integral part of our competitive edge. We've designed tools that:

- reduce the time it takes to index court documents from hours to minutes
- streamline and largely automate the preparation of complex affidavits
- define intelligent workflows, processes and decision trees for routine work
- completely automate tedious tasks like checking death notices and conflict searches.

Then we have alternative legal service providers (ALSPs), who are exploiting technology to provide services far more efficiently and cost effectively than traditional lawyers. They've jumped to fill a gap in the market that most lawyers are missing as they're too focused on the practice of law.

The challenge facing the profession has been neatly described as the more-for-less challenge, which is exactly as its name suggests: clients are demanding more but are willing to pay less.

No doubt you've experienced this yourself with the needy litigant who wants an experienced representative at the price of a junior, or the client who wants a discount on your already low-cost service because they can get a template online for free. Of course, the fact that you're offering a customised document prepared specifically for their needs seems to be beside the point.

Today, law is a buyer's market. To succeed in this market, you need to recognise the power shift, accept that you're no longer calling the shots, and set about finding better ways to provide value.

As Furlong explains:

> *The law firms that make it through this coming decade, therefore, will be sophisticated, productive, multi-dimensional businesses that organize and apply legal expertise to deliver value to buyers with maximum effectiveness ... they will have fewer lawyers than they once did and will rely more on processes and technology. They're not going to be run like country clubs, money machines, or boutique hotels for lawyers who are more interested in their own affairs than those of the firm. They will choose to become strong, professional, buyer-first businesses, and will take the steps necessary to achieve that goal.*

WHAT DOES THIS MEAN FOR YOU?

There's no longer a debate about whether the legal industry will change; the simple answer is that it already has. The old, established way of practising law is being questioned and rejected by both lawyers and clients. We're facing what's been dubbed the 'uberisation' of law. Just as Uber disrupted the traditional taxi service, new business models and technology are disrupting the traditional law firm business model.

You know this already, but it's time to face it head on. Look into the future of law and aim there, not to recreate the past. Burying your head in the sand won't get you anywhere.

KEY POINTS IN THIS CHAPTER

1. The power has shifted. Lawyers are no longer calling the shots. Law is a buyer's market.

2. Clients have easy access to more information than ever before. They are educated about their legal issue before they pick up the phone or send you an email. This has changed their expectations of legal services. They don't want to pay for information, they want solutions.

3. Technology is transforming the nature of legal services to make them more efficient and effective.

4. The more-for-less challenge sees client demands increasing at the same time as their budgets are tightening. To thrive in the future of law, you need to address this challenge.

The journey to Productise and Profit

'The difficulty lies, not in the new ideas, but in escaping
from old ones.'

John Maynard Keynes

By now, two things are clear. First, you need to start treating your law firm like a business. Second, you need to do business on your clients' terms.

But what does that change look like?

Transforming the way your business operates isn't going to happen overnight. It's a journey that will include shifts in attitudes, values, mindsets, ways of thinking and ways of working, all of which will snowball as you begin the journey and continue to build momentum. It will lead you to an entirely new way of running your business, but it isn't a single event. You won't wake up one day and find yourself in a new business.

But if you follow my Productise and Profit model, you can be confident you'll make progress towards living the life you want and stop letting your law practice overwhelm your life.

One of the keys to Productise and Profit is to transform your *services* into *products*. I know – confusing right? I'll explain how to do this in step three, but for now, you need to know that a productised service has a predefined scope, a fixed price and a system or method for delivery. Before I explain the Productise and Profit model, I want to give you a glimpse of the journey ahead.

THE FIVE STAGES OF LAW FIRM DEVELOPMENT

In my experience, law firms typically find themselves in one of five stages:

1. traditional
2. limited scope
3. specialist
4. productised services
5. product ecosystem.

These are shown in the following table.

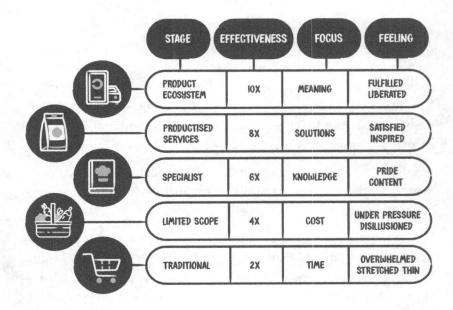

STAGE	EFFECTIVENESS	FOCUS	FEELING
PRODUCT ECOSYSTEM	10X	MEANING	FULFILLED LIBERATED
PRODUCTISED SERVICES	8X	SOLUTIONS	SATISFIED INSPIRED
SPECIALIST	6X	KNOWLEDGE	PRIDE CONTENT
LIMITED SCOPE	4X	COST	UNDER PRESSURE DISILLUSIONED
TRADITIONAL	2X	TIME	OVERWHELMED STRETCHED THIN

Where you are on this spectrum will affect how you feel about your business, how much money you're making, and what steps you should be taking next.

Before you get started with Productise and Profit, consider what stage you're at now.

Stage one: traditional practice

We all know how traditional legal services work. They look a bit like this:

You list your practice areas, skills and expertise and aim to provide a customised service for every client. Chances are, you never turn down work, even if it's something you're not very good at or don't really know how to do. Why? Because turning down work means turning down money, and you can never be sure when the next client will come through the door. As a result, your service offering gets wider, as does that niggling feeling in the back of your mind that you'll miss something or make a mistake.

Every client demands a different service, so you have no systems to guide you. After all, you can't create a system for something that you've never done before. At stage one, you are the supermarket, offering all things to all customers.

You sell services on a timed basis, and because of this, time is the focus of everything you do. You *think* you're on the right track, because we're all told that lawyers sell time in six-minute units, but you can't shake that feeling that there's a better way. You can't escape your business, because your income is directly linked to your time. If you're not recording minutes on a time sheet, you're not making money.

You feel overwhelmed and stretched thin. Sooner or later you'll reach a ceiling because you'll be maxed out. You've reached capacity, but the good news is that you've recognised that there must be a better way.

Stage two: limited scope

In stage two, you decide to try limited scope services. You take a group of services, bundle them together and put a price on them. That price, though, is just a function of the number of hours you think the work will take you multiplied by your hourly rate and, really, that's just hourly billing by another name.

You're still selling deliverables – 'We will do x, y and z' – not outcomes.

At stage two, you've changed from a supermarket to a fruit and veg delivery box. You give your client different ingredients, but they have to work out how they fit together. Even though you've got some limited scope packages, you're still 'full service'. You go to lengths to explain that, as well as the delivery box, clients can add in anything else they like. Need some juice, bread or toilet roll? No problem.

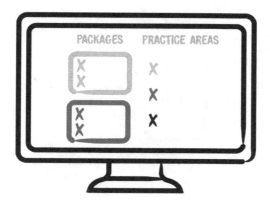

You feel under pressure and disillusioned. You're stuck between the old and the new. You know what you want to be doing, but fear and uncertainty hold you back and you struggle to say no to work that you don't really want to do.

Stage three: specialist

After a while you decide to embrace your expertise and specialty. You see how effective your limited scope services are compared to everything else, so you stop offering anything to anyone who asks and you start to focus on refining your niche. You spend time getting to understand the people you serve. You learn about their problems, fears and desires.

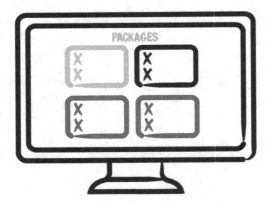

You design services based on customer research, needs and feedback. You start to develop systems to govern service delivery. When you carry out a service, you ask yourself how you can leverage that knowledge so you can use it again. You charge for your services at fixed prices, and realise that you make more profit this way than when you charged by time. After all, do you pay the tradesperson for the time it takes to use the hammer or for knowing where to hit?

Now, you're Hello Fresh. You deliver the ingredients for a specific recipe. You've realised that your time is not your commodity, and you want to leverage your knowledge even more.

Stage four: productised services

The way to get that leverage is to *productise your services*.

Think home delivery from your favourite restaurant. You deliver a complete solution to your client's problem. A cooked meal, delivered to their door. You're no longer listing skills and expertise, you're taking your clients from problem to solution in a systemised way.

You offer a specific type of service for a specific type of client. You're not scrambling to learn the latest developments in a practice area you haven't touched for 10 years. Your productised services make it easy to attract, convert and deliver. You offer tangible solutions, not a list of skills.

Your products are packaged solutions to your clients' problems, sold at a fixed price. Your systems are automated, you lead a high-performing and effective team, and you get to spend your time on the parts of the work you love.

You feel satisfied and inspired with what you do.

Stage five: product ecosystem

Stage five is the ultimate in meal delivery: Uber Eats. An entire menu of complementary products. Clients can choose their cuisine, add in a dessert, and the meals will be delivered to their door.

In your law firm, you have a whole ecosystem of products – flagship and bespoke – that work together to create a thriving business. Each product works in harmony with the others. Together, the products maximise value and increase demand.

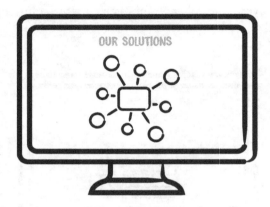

Your focus is on doing *meaningful work* – your systems let you eliminate the grunt work and enable you to focus on the parts of the service that really require your brain power. You only do work you love. The best part, though, is that this thriving ecosystem isn't dependent on you. You have time for all the other priorities in life.

WHICH STAGE ARE YOU IN?

Do you relate to any of these stages?

There's no right or wrong. Most people who pick up this book are in the traditional stage, perhaps with one foot in the limited scope camp.

Wherever you are, what does it feel like for you? Do you relate to the feelings I've shared?

Think about where you are and where you're headed. What will it feel like when you reach that goal? How will that change your business, your family and your life?

This book provides a proven step-by-step blueprint to take you from a traditional practice to a product ecosystem that lets you regain your life.

THE FOUR ELEMENTS TO LAW FIRM SUCCESS

Running a successful law firm business in the modern economy requires you to focus your efforts at the intersection of four areas: the practice of law, the business of law, legal operations and people.

Let's take a look at each of these.

The practice of law

This one is self-explanatory. Your business must be founded on a deep understanding of the law. You must have the legal knowledge and skills to deliver legal services and to practise law.

The business of law

There's still some resistance to the idea that law firms are businesses. The concern seems to be that when we treat our practice like a business, our motive shifts from the administration of justice to making a profit. I'd argue that a business model that is built on selling units of time for a high hourly rate, with no measure of the effectiveness of those minutes, is already centred on profit. It certainly isn't centred on delivering the best outcome for the client. Understanding the business of law means thinking much more broadly than simply exchanging time for money. The business of law is about:

- business planning and strategy

- understanding alternative business models

- pricing and alternative fee arrangements

- financial management – understanding the costs of running the business, revenue, cash flow and profit

- modern marketing, positioning and business branding

- people, team building, leadership and culture

- client service and experience

- continuous improvement, including leveraging knowledge, systems and processes.

Legal operations

Legal operations looks at how to make a law firm run more efficiently and effectively. The legal operations function began in in-house legal departments in response to the more-for-less challenge – the increasing demand for legal services that coincides with pressure to control costs – but is just as relevant for law firms like yours.

Typical roles and responsibilities of legal operations include:

- define and improve systems and processes

- implement new technology to achieve the business's goals

- optimise law firm performance

- intellectual property and knowledge management

- standardisation and automation of repetitive or administrative tasks.

It's important to make sure these skills exist within your team, regardless of whether you have a dedicated legal operations department or manager.

People

Ultimately, law is about human relationships, so it should come as no surprise that people are a pillar for success. As a small law firm owner, you need to consider 'people' from three perspectives: yourself, your staff and your clients. There is a push for a more human-centric practice of law, and the 'people' pillar recognises this.

* * *

Each of these four elements has equal weight. If you want to Productise and Profit, you need to address all four.

You may be the best lawyer in town, but if you don't understand the business of running a law firm and you make no effort to improve your business operations, your success will always be limited by your hourly rate multiplied by the number of hours you bill. Likewise, you can run the most efficient law firm in town, but if you don't have a good understanding of the people you serve, clients won't be interested in buying your service.

The elements are not linear, they are circular, and each element depends on each of the others. You might need to place different emphasis on each of the elements at different times and for different purposes, but no one element in isolation will lead you to success.

KEY POINTS IN THIS CHAPTER

1. Building a product ecosystem that gives you the lifestyle you want won't happen overnight, it's a journey that will transform your business and your life.

2. You'll progress through five stages: traditional law, limited scope, specialist, productised services and, finally, product ecosystem.

3. Running a successful law firm business in the modern economy requires you to focus your efforts at the intersection of four areas: the practice of law, the business of law, legal operations and people.

How to implement Productise and Profit in your firm

'Entrepreneurship is about turning what excites you in life into capital, so that you can do more of it and move forward with it.'

Richard Branson

PRODUCTISE AND PROFIT is a six-stage blueprint for making your law firm more efficient and effective so you can regain control, have a successful business and also have time for all the other priorities in your life. You'll learn how to transform your law firm from a traditional practice to a productised ecosystem that gives you the lifestyle you want.

Profit is about much more than financial profit. Of course you want to profit financially from your business, and if you follow this model you will. But Profit is also about all the other things you want more of: time, enjoyment, joy, meaning and impact.

Here are the stages we'll work through:

| FIND YOUR VISION | DEEPLY UNDERSTAND YOUR CLIENTS | CREATE AMAZING SOLUTIONS | PRODUCTISE YOUR SERVICES | EMBRACE MODERN MARKETING | OPTIMISE YOUR OPERATIONS |

The order of the steps is important, so try not to jump ahead. I will finish each step with an action plan telling you how to implement the ideas in the chapter and 'do law differently'.

It's time to jump into the driver's seat and take control of your business.

Let's do it.

Step 1:
Find your vision

'A lifestyle change begins with a vision and a single step.'

Jeff Galloway

FIND YOUR VISION | DEEPLY UNDERSTAND YOUR CLIENTS | CREATE AMAZING SOLUTIONS | PRODUCTISE YOUR SERVICES | EMBRACE MODERN MARKETING | OPTIMISE YOUR OPERATIONS

A BIG QUESTION

What do you want your life to look like?

It's a big question. How would you answer it?

Whenever I ask this question I'm met with two different kinds of responses. The first are people who *absolutely* know what they want. They start listing all the elements of their ideal life, from how much time they spend with their kids to where they live, what they do at work and for leisure, and how much money they earn. They paint a picture so vivid I can see it in my own mind. All that's left is to map out the path to help them get there.

The second group are almost the total opposite. They stare blankly at me, stunned. They're so overwhelmed with work that they feel the choice about how they live their life has been taken away from them. The vision of 'work–life balance' they had when they started their business is a distant memory. They feel like they have no control over what today looks like, let alone the rest of their life.

What about you? What do you want *your* life to look like?

Think about your answer, because the starting point for reshaping your business has nothing to do with business and everything to do with you. If you're going to redesign your business, you might as well make it one you love.

First, you need to work out what you want your life to look like. Then you can set about building a business that lets you live that life.

SCALE IS NOT A DESTINATION

In *How The Mighty Fall*, Jim Collins describes the five stages that once great companies pass through on their decline. Stage two is the 'Undisciplined pursuit of more', where companies want more of whatever it is that those in power define as success. Growth for growth's sake is not a good strategy and, according to Collins, is the beginning of the end. Big is not the same as great, and neither is bigger necessarily more profitable.

But I don't have to scroll far on my Facebook feed until I'm met with an ad promising to help me scale or build a seven-figure business. We're bombarded with messages telling us to scale, to grow and to want more, more, more. It's easy to become caught up in that narrative, but I encourage you to take a minute to really consider if it's right for you. You don't *have* to want more, nor do you have to buy into the economic model of success.

Don't get me wrong; I'm not saying you shouldn't earn a good income, just that it shouldn't be your only definition of success. Most of the people I work with to help them redesign their businesses aren't chasing world domination. Yes, they want to build a successful business that they enjoy, that makes a difference in the world, and that makes a decent profit. But then they want to switch off, spend time with their families, travel, and live outside of work without feeling the pressure of running a business 24/7. Building an empire of massive proportions rarely features on the wishlist.

Is it *more* you're chasing? Or are you just after a better lifestyle?

A BIRD'S EYE VIEW

To help them take a bird's eye view of all the components of their life, I get my coaching clients to complete a Wheel of Life by rating their satisfaction with each area of their life from 0 to 10, as shown below.

The Wheel of Life

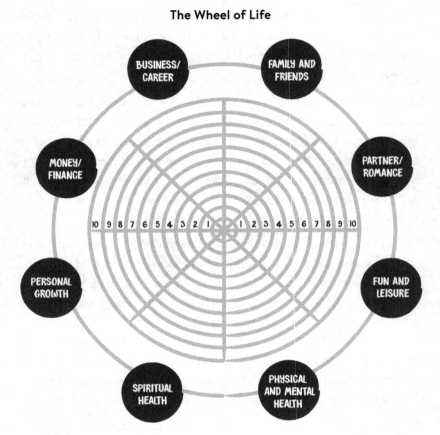

By visualising all the areas of life at once, the wheel helps you to understand where your life is flourishing and which areas need more work.

One client reflected that, except for her business, her wheel was deflated. The exercise helped her realise she was spending all her time on her business and not prioritising family and friends, fun or physical health. The Wheel of Life was the penny-drop moment that helped her see the way she was running her business wasn't giving her the lifestyle she'd intended after all.

What does *your* ideal lifestyle look like? Maybe you want to work school hours so you can pick the kids up every day, or perhaps you just want to be able to switch off on the weekends and go paddle boarding without having that unfinished to-do list ruining your pleasure? You get to decide this, but you need to know what you're aiming for.

YOU HAVE A BLANK SLATE

I host the Doing Law Differently podcast, on which I interview leaders of law firms from around Australia about how they're breaking the traditional law mould and, well, *doing law differently*. A theme that comes up time and time again is the idea of starting a law firm with a blank slate.

Many people start their own law firm because they're unhappy with the traditional law model. Somewhere on the journey from employment to entrepreneurship they realise that they don't have to do things the way they've always been done.

Sean King, Director of Proximity – a professional services business providing legal, commercial and consulting services to the government and regulated industry sector – told me how he and his co-director actively sat down and asked themselves what they wanted to keep from traditional law and what they'd leave behind.[1]

Family and Surrogacy lawyer Sarah Jefford told me how empowered she felt when she realised she could do business on her terms, and she set about creating a business that she loves so much it doesn't feel like work.[2]

This opportunity is yours too. You can KonMari your way through your business, keeping only the things that spark joy and discarding

---

1   Listen to Sean King explain this on episode 58 of the Doing Law Differently podcast.
2   You can hear Sarah's story on episode 57 of the Doing Law Differently podcast.

the rest (after you thank them for their service, of course). You don't have to do things the way they've always been done. You can reshape your law firm to serve your lifestyle, not take from it.

BRING MORE JOY TO YOUR WORK

Ikigai is a Japanese concept that means 'a reason for being'. Ikigai looks at four areas to identify your purpose:

1. What you love.

2. What the world needs.

3. What you're good at.

4. What you can be paid for.

The ultimate goal is to find the intersection between these four elements. Ikigai is about integrating all the components of life. When we know our ikigai and when we spend our time on things that are meaningful to us we experience a greater sense of joy.

Sarah Jefford has designed her business as an expression of her ikigai. She is an IVF mum, egg donor and surrogate. Surrogacy is her passion, and is now also the focus of her business. She KonMaried the rest and left only what sparked joy. She is now the only lawyer in Australia practising exclusively in surrogacy and donor conception (family creation) law. She's written a book and hosts a successful podcast on the topic, creative outlets that she loves more than the law itself, but that she's able to do because she designed her business in a way that gives her time to do them.

Maybe your passion doesn't cross over with your business quite so perfectly, but you can still carve out the things you enjoy. We continually refine our services to remove the work that doesn't bring us joy.

Michael Hodgkins, Director at Birman & Ride, decided that he didn't like contested family law, so he stopped offering that service and instead created Resolution Family Law, a niche business that provides legal services to separating couples who need help formalising an agreement that they've already reached. Over the years we've removed other services from our offering too. Retail shop leases were the first to go. The laws changed more frequently than we delivered the service, which meant we were always playing catch up and for very little profit. More recently we removed three entire practice areas from our firm. The product ecosystems we've built in other practice areas provide plenty of work to keep us happy, engaged and make a decent profit, so we applied the 80–20 rule and chopped off the bottom of our service menu.

Now is as good a time as any to think about how you can bring more of what you love into your business.

YOUR BUSINESS VISION

Once you've spent some time thinking about what you want your life to look like and how to bring more joy to your work, you can then work out how to translate that into a vision for your business. The goal is to design a business that gives you the life you want.

Simon Sinek is best known for popularising the concept of 'why' in his 2009 TED Talk and book *Start with Why: How great leaders inspire everyone to take action*. Sinek encourages business owners to understand and communicate *why* they do what they do (their purpose) over and above *what* they do (the products or services they sell) and *how* they do it (things that set them apart from their competitors). He says that a business's purpose isn't about making money, but about a cause or belief that's the very reason an organisation exists.

According to Sinek, 'people don't buy what you do, they buy why you do it'. To drive good decision making, we need to communicate from the inside-out. We need to start with why.

Understanding your why is an important foundation block to a successful business. Your why tells others not just who you are, but what you're about, what you stand for and what they can expect from you.

It also acts as a filter through which you can pass future opportunities to assess whether they're right for you. It will help with prioritisation, decision-making, motivating yourself and others, and pulling through the hard times.

You'd be hard pressed to find a lawyer who doesn't tell you that they started their career with a desire to 'help people', but dig deeper than this. I asked a group of lawyers to tell me their business's 'why'. Here are some of them:

- Make legal services more accessible to the missing middle, those who earn too much to access legal aid, but not enough to afford the legal services they need.

- To simplify the divorce process for separating families.

- To help employers to create a thriving team.

- To create a happy, supporting and effective legal environment so that we can all sleep better at night.

- To allow people access to quick, speedy, commercial outcomes from their business disputes – and to give them the skills to avoid their disputes from escalating.

KNOW YOUR ENDGAME

Every journey starts with a destination in mind, whether it's sailing to the Bahamas, a road trip around Australia, or even your morning jog. Your law firm is no exception. Knowing your endgame will help keep you motivated.

This book gives you the guidance you need to reshape your firm and regain your life, but without knowing what you want your life to look like, what good will it do?

The goal is to intentionally design your business to fit your purpose, your vision and your life. Build your business, not someone else's. After all, that's why you started your law firm in the first place, isn't it?

KEY POINTS IN THIS CHAPTER

1. This is an opportunity to reshape your business to suit your life. What do you want your life to look like?

2. Scale is not a destination. Don't get caught up in the narrative telling you to grow if growth isn't what you really want. Remember, big isn't the same as great.

3. Spend some time understanding why you do what you do. Having a business purpose will not only help frame future opportunities, it will also help potential clients understand what you stand for.

 ## IT'S TIME TO DO LAW DIFFERENTLY

- Develop a vision for your life. What do you want your life to look like? Complete The Wheel of Life exercise to rate your happiness with each area of life. How bumpy is your ride?

- How can you do more of what you love in your business?

- Identify what parts of your business no longer spark joy. How can you remove them?

- Understand your why.

Step 2:
Deeply understand your clients

'Could a greater miracle take place than for us to look through each other's eyes for an instant?'

Henry David Thoreau, Author

FIND YOUR VISION | DEEPLY UNDERSTAND YOUR CLIENTS | CREATE AMAZING SOLUTIONS | PRODUCTISE YOUR SERVICES | EMBRACE MODERN MARKETING | OPTIMISE YOUR OPERATIONS

Now you've got your vision sorted, the next step is to know your clients better than they know themselves. I want you to understand every aspect of the people you work for. Not just their legal issues, I'm talking what motivates them? How do they like to spend their time? What keeps them awake at night?

If you think this has nothing to do with your legal services, you're wrong.

When you have a deep understanding of the people you serve and use this as your starting point, you'll end with innovative solutions that are tailor made to suit their needs. You'll effortlessly create products and services that your clients will embrace. When you combine your client-centric services (steps three and four) with some excellent positioning and marketing (step five), you'll become a client magnet. No longer will you need to spend time chasing new work, the right kind of work will come to you.

The best part, though, is the realisation that you have the power to choose who you work for. The cab-rank rule doesn't apply to lawyers. Not everyone is your client, and nor do you want them to be. You have real power as a business owner to find clients who want what you offer, in the way you do it and at the price you need them to pay. While targeting your efforts like this might seem scary, it will be worth it – for your business and your life.

I recently coached a sole practitioner, let's call her Gabriella, who needed help with her law firm's positioning. She'd been running her practice for six years, and during that time she'd never marketed her business. All her work came from referrals. It's a great position to be in, except that taking referral work meant she'd take on anything and everything that came her way. She was doing a huge variety of work – from commercial litigation to drafting wills, tax advice and family provision claims. She wanted to build a business that let her do more of the things she loved and less of the things she didn't. When I asked her to describe the people she helped, like most lawyers, she replied with 'anyone who needs my advice'. She went on to tell me that she worked for tradies, professional workers, mums and dads, mortgage brokers and engineering companies. When I asked her to find the common thread, she struggled.

In 2010, we started to segment our market. We created separate brand names and flagship products for most of the firm's primary markets. If a potential client needs a will, they're more likely to consider a business called 'Perth Wills Centre' than they are 'Birman & Ride', who also provide myriad other services.

Harvard Business School professor Clayton Christensen describes the approach of building an entire brand around a job to be done as 'purpose branding'. Purpose branding involves naming the product after the purpose it serves. In other words, as Clarissa Rayward, Director of Brisbane Family Law Centre, likes to say, it does what it says on the tin.

There's nothing wrong with having a variety of clients, but it makes better business sense to focus your energy on a particular group of people. The problem with helping *anyone* is that your message becomes diluted. In your attempt to serve everyone, you do a disservice to the people who need you most. By offering any service to anyone who asks you're adding to your workload and risking exhaustion. You can't please everyone, and nor should you try to. The greater clarity you have about who you serve, the more focused and effective your business will be.

It seems counterintuitive to design services that appeal to a small, specialised section of the population, but a narrow focus on core business sustains profit and growth. In a world where information is free, vast and openly accessible, clients are looking for a lawyer who knows how to take that information and apply it to create a valuable solution. According to the 2019 *NAB Australian Legal Services Industry Survey*, 83% of businesses said that niche expertise was the reason they considered a law firm, and 51% saw it as a clincher in their purchasing decision.[1]

Think about it. If you need neurosurgery, you see a neurologist, not a general surgeon. If you have toothache, you go to a dentist, not a GP. If you need your garden tidied, you'll seek out a gardener, not a handyman. Legal services are no different.

Carving out a niche market and positioning your business as the go-to helps build your credibility. It's an excellent way to differentiate your business and help potential clients recognise you as the firm they need to solve their legal problems. Having a narrow focus means you can concentrate your resources on your core business.

Narrowing your range of services or the type of clients you target feels risky. No one hates turning down work more than a small business owner. If someone wants to pay you to do something, why wouldn't you? Chances are, though, when you break it down, work you're not an expert at is not profitable and, in the legal profession especially, is risky too. It typically costs much more to serve the needs of a broad market of clients or offer a broad variety of services than it does to have a narrow market or range of services. Not every dollar is created equally. Sometimes you'll be better off saying no to the cash and investing the time in improving your productised services or working on your marketing strategy to sell more of what you're good at. This is exactly the reason why we do a regular clear out of our services.

---

1   business.nab.com.au/wp-content/uploads/2019/08/NAB-Legal-Services-Industry-Survey.pdf.

As Steve Jobs famously said:

> *People think focus means saying yes to the thing you've got to focus on. But that's not what it means at all. It means saying no to the 100 other good ideas that there are. You have to pick carefully. I'm actually as proud of the many things we at Apple haven't done, as the things we have done.*

THE POWER OF EMPATHY

Human-centred design is a philosophy that empowers people designing products or services to do so with the intention of solving a problem or improving an aspect of the consumer's life. Unlike traditional methods of creating services that focus on the problem, human-centred design focuses on the people who have the problem.

Lawyers are increasingly looking to the design industry to help them reinvent the way they provide services.

For designers, empathy is key. In their *Field Guide to Human-Centered Design*, global design company IDEO explain empathy as a 'deep understanding of the problems and realities of the people you are designing for'. Empathy is your ability to see the world through other people's eyes.

By setting aside your own assumptions and taking the time to develop understandings, experiences, insights and observations about the people you serve, you will come up with solutions that create real impact.

HOW TO UNDERSTAND YOUR IDEAL CLIENT

1. Knowing who you help is the essential first step

There are plenty of strategies and tools you can use to map a profile of your ideal client, but knowing who they are can be a tricky first step.

Have you ever stopped to question who you're trying to help? If your answer is 'no', don't worry, you're not alone. University segments law into subjects and practice areas that tend to follow us into practice. As a result, most lawyers focus on what they have to offer. So, if it helps to get you started, start there. Consider what problem you're trying to solve with the services you sell.

Let's say you're an employment lawyer and you love to help small business owners learn how to effectively manage and engage their team. The problems your clients are experiencing might be a lack of understanding about their legal obligations when it comes to employment, the inability to find or attract the right staff, or lacking the knowledge or skills to manage different people.

Once you've identified the problem you solve, you can then start to think about the demographics and psychographics of the people you're trying to help and dig deeper to learn more about what it is they really want.

If you're still unsure, let me ask you this: if you had the chance to scrap your current client list and work only with people you wanted to work with, who would make the cut? What type of people do you want to help, and what problems do you want to help them with? If you could only work for one client, who would it be?

Would you keep Joe the plumber who sends you work weekly, but the work is low value and Joe is high maintenance, demanding that only you take his calls and refusing to deal with any juniors? What about the company who engages you to do regular but low-level work that's boring but pays well? Or the business owner who takes up all your resources for a month at a time, but it's work you love?

Brisbane Family Law Centre help people going through separation and divorce who value their relationships with others above anything else. They do so in a way that keeps them outside of the family law courts and enables them to be friends. It's clear that the disgruntled wife looking to sue her ex-husband for everything he's got isn't going to be a good fit for BFLC.

Or try it another way: if you were to ask a friend to refer business to you, how would you describe the characteristics of the people your business is aimed at helping?

Nest Legal are 'lawyers for busy people'. Their clients are people whose lifestyles don't allow them to wait around in a lawyer's office. Nest know their clients are busy, so they offer services in ways that appeal to busy people, including offering after-hours video and phone consultations and keeping toys and snacks in their office to entertain children who come along to appointments with their parents.[2]

When you've figured out who your ideal client is, your next step is to understand everything you can about them.

2. What are your ideal client's demographics and psychographics?

Start by considering their demographics, including their:

- age
- sex
- marital status
- number of children (if any)
- location
- education level
- employment status
- occupation

---

2   Learn more about Nest Legal in my interview with founder, Laura Vickers on episode 16 of the Doing Law Differently podcast.

- income level

- religion

- race.

You can also consider the psychographic traits of your ideal client to help you understand their attitudes, personality, values and interests. Consider:

- What are their interests?

- What are their hobbies?

- What do they value the most?

- What are they afraid to lose?

- Who or what do they trust for advice?

- How do they make a decision?

- Do they use social media platforms? Which ones, and what for?

Whether your clients are individuals or businesses, we all do business with people, and people are motivated by many different desires.

What really motivates them? What is the trigger point? What is the point at which they decide 'enough is enough', and they commit to taking action to address their problems? They may be motivated by what they have to gain, but also consider what they've got to lose.

Motivation is always made up of a number of factors, so it can be hard to pinpoint. Mapping your ideal client's traits on a spectrum can help you understand what factors might influence their willingness to buy your service to solve their problem.

Consider criteria relevant to your ideal client – for example:

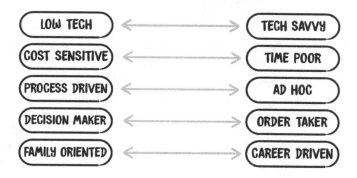

3. What's your ideal client's biggest problem?

Next, dig deeper on the problems your ideal clients have. Don't limit yourself to what you *perceive* as their legal problems or *expect* them to be. Instead, consider their life or business problems more generally. What is the human problem that sits underneath the law? When you think more broadly, you'll open up whole new avenues you'd never before considered.

Start by brainstorming their *public problems*. These are the things they'll openly admit to others. It might be that they need a will to make sure their estate is divided in accordance with their wishes, or perhaps they need to sell their business but have no idea where to start.

Next, think about their *private problems*. What's the part they're holding back? Think about the problems they save for their closest friends and confidants. Maybe it's that they want to leave one of their children out of the will, or they're worried that if they don't sell the business now, soon it will be worthless, and they'll be left with mounds of debt.

Then go deeper still and look below the surface for their *unspoken problems*. What keeps them awake at night? The fallout and family breakdown when their children learn they won't receive any inheritance? Or the fear about how they'll support their family if their business goes under?

Breaking a problem down into these three levels can help you to really understand your clients on a deeper level. People don't always share all the details. You might need to read between the lines or look for what is not said in order to find the insights that will make the most meaningful difference.

Take this book, for example. Your problems are that you're busy doing legal work and don't have time to work *on* your business, that you feel frustrated doing the grunt work over and over, that your days are full of interruptions from staff and clients, and that you can't even take a week off without everything coming tumbling down.

Those are the practical challenges, but the problems that keep you awake at night are different. Those are questions like 'will my business survive?', and feeling guilty over not spending as much time with your kids as you'd like.

It is these unspoken challenges that people will connect with. If you can become part of the conversation your ideal clients are having in their own head, you'll get instant cut-through.

4. Ask, don't assume

I remember my first day at our law firm like it was yesterday. I'd carefully chosen what to wear, making sure to buy myself new shoes that had a heel that was high, but not too high, a fresh black blazer with sleeves too long so that I had to fold them up, and a spare pair of tights in my bag – heaven forbid I'd get a ladder. I was one of three law students showing up for day one of the firm's cadetship program. We spent the entire first day in the boardroom with both of the firm's partners. There was a bowl of jelly beans in the middle of the table, but we were all so on edge that I don't think any of us ate them.

We spent the first two days being drilled in a training session they affectionately named 'bootcamp.' Bootcamp was designed to teach us many of the things we needed to know about how to conduct ourselves in law land. I learned many of my most valuable lessons that day. From how to shake hands and introduce myself to knowing never to go anywhere without a pen and file note, how to calculate GST, and to always bring flat shoes in case I needed a mad dash to court. One of the lessons that stuck with me was to never assume – 'when you assume you make an ASS out of U and ME'.

No doubt the exercises in this chapter will enlighten you and help you to discover a lot you didn't know about your clients, and maybe after doing them you're already brimming with ideas about how you can help them in new ways, but don't make the mistake of stopping there. Don't assume you've got it right. In fact, chances are you haven't. In the 2019 *NAB Australian Legal Services Industry Survey*, NAB found that 26% of SMEs changed law firms because they felt that their current provider didn't understand their business.

Now you know who your ideal clients are, I'm going to tell you to do something completely wild.

Talk to them and ask them what they need.

Pick up the phone, arrange a meeting, and spend time getting to really know your clients. Ask them about the questions you've considered in this chapter.

If you can't bring yourself to ask someone you don't know, start with your existing clients. Next time you speak to a client on the phone, ask them to spend a few minutes helping you understand more about their problem. Even a question as simple as 'why did you choose to engage me?' can open up a wealth of valuable knowledge.

As you talk, listen for insights into how they make decisions, what motivates them, what their pain points are, what's frustrating them and what's holding them back. Ask questions that relate to them, not you. Your aim is to understand your clients and their problems, not get validation for your services – that will come later.

*　*　*

The process of identifying potential clients and working out how to meet their needs is known as 'customer development'. The aim is to make sure you create services that people actually want by assessing demand before they're developed. In her book *Lean Customer Development: Build products your customers need*, Cindy Alvarez describes customer development as a 'shift in perspective away from building a better product and toward building a more successful customer'.

By testing your idea through customer development, you can avoid spending time and money on creating something that no one wants. Put another way, it avoids making an ass of u and me.

It's human nature to be biased towards our own good ideas. We have a tendency to assume that because we're experts at the law, we understand what our clients need and how they want it. Sometimes we might be right, but often we'll be wrong.

A couple of years ago we thought it would be a great idea to sell conveyancing services to our family law clients. They were going through a separation, and the majority of them needed some type of property transfer as part of their property settlement. We packaged a service that included consent orders and a property transfer and tried to convince prospective clients that they should buy the package now. We could be a 'one-stop-shop'; they could complete the whole property settlement in one fell swoop. Trouble was, no one bought it. Yes, they all needed the service, but at the time when they engaged us, conveyancing was not on their radar. Many of them were yet to work out who'd keep the house, let alone think about the legalities of the property transfer. Practically speaking, it made sense; but from the client's perspective, they had no interest in buying the service in that way. When we changed focus and started to offer the service later in the process, we saw a much bigger uptake.

Customer development forces us to get out of our own heads and understand our clients. When we do so, we quickly learn what it is that they want and, importantly, what they'll pay for.

PUT THE CUSTOMER FIRST, PROFITS WILL COME

Think about your business today. How many of your clients meet the profile of your ideal client? My guess is that it's less than half, probably far less. Imagine how your business would look if your entire client base was made up of your ideal clients.

I know this prospect is equally as daunting as it is exciting. No business owner likes the idea of turning down work. But having an ideal client doesn't mean you're never going to work for anybody else. Instead, it serves as an anchor from which you can design your services and position your marketing. One of the most important things you can do in business is to clearly identify the best client for your product or service, and then focus everything you do on that type of person.

A successful entrepreneur sees a business as a system for producing results for the customer which result in profits for the business. Without a clear picture of the customer, no business can succeed.

Understanding your client's needs and solving their problems is the most foolproof way to business certainty.

By the end of my session with Gabriella, we'd nutted out her ideal client. As it turns out, she didn't really want to help everyone at all, and when she stopped to think about it, nor did she really enjoy a lot of the work she was doing day to day. The work she loved was advising on contested estates. The problems her ideal clients had were that they'd found themselves in the middle of a family fight and they wanted out, but they also wanted to fight for what they thought was fair. They needed an advisor who could be rational, try to take some of the emotion out, and help resolve the conflict. Gabriella loved working with what we called sophisticated professionals, middle-to-high-income earners who, in her experience, were receptive to her advice, had reasonable expectations of what legal outcomes could be achieved, and with whom she had a relationship of mutual respect. Just like that, we'd narrowed Gabriella's focus.

Her question now became how she'd design her solutions, and position and market herself so she could start doing more of what she loved and less of what she didn't. In turn, she'd stop feeling so overwhelmed. She wouldn't have to be across so many different areas of law and she'd be working with people she enjoyed being around.

KEY POINTS IN THIS CHAPTER

1. Customer centricity is the key to business success. Who is your ideal client and how are you solving their problems?

2. Human-centred design requires you to shift your focus from what you do to the people whose problems you solve.

3. You don't have to accept any and all work that comes through the door. When you've built your business machine, you can work with only the people you choose.

4. When considering your client's problems, think bigger than law. This will open up new opportunities.

 ## IT'S TIME TO DO LAW DIFFERENTLY

- Decide who your ideal client is.

- Spend time understanding their problems – what do they really want?

- Don't assume you've got it right. Talk to your clients to validate your assumptions.

Step 3:
Create amazing solutions

'Don't find customers for your products, find products for your customers.'

Seth Godin

FIND YOUR VISION   DEEPLY UNDERSTAND YOUR CLIENTS   CREATE AMAZING SOLUTIONS   PRODUCTISE YOUR SERVICES   EMBRACE MODERN MARKETING   OPTIMISE YOUR OPERATIONS

Sorry to break it to you – your clients don't care about your qualifications.

Let's face it, no one sees a lawyer for fun. Maybe they've found themselves caught up in a family dispute over an inheritance, or perhaps they need help to protect their business against someone else's unlawful use of their trademark. Whatever the reason, they see you because they're reacting to or trying to avoid a legal problem, or they have a serious personal or financial goal they're trying to achieve.

Although they need your help, most aren't interested in your qualifications, and they sure as hell aren't interested in buying your time.

So what do they want?

They want a solution to their problem.

Understanding the distinction is important. Making the switch from selling your *expertise* to selling a *product that will solve your clients' problem* will transform your business.

Most lawyers' websites offer little more than a list of practice areas and staff capabilities. I did a Google search for 'family lawyer' and looked at the results. Many of them had home pages that looked something like this:

We handle all family law matters:

- dispute resolution
- settlement agreements
- parenting plans and orders
- child support
- custody issues
- court process
- de facto separation
- divorce

- property settlements
- estate planning
- spousal maintenance
- superannuation.

Compare that with this alternative from South Australian law firm, Resolve Divorce:

> *At Resolve Divorce, we specialise in achieving legal outcomes that focus on your overall wellbeing, which helps achieve a better settlement for you and your family.*
>
> *We help to navigate the legal process of separation and divorce through an approach that encourages mutually beneficial compromise without the negativity or emotional toll of traditional pathways.*
>
> *Our experienced and qualified team strive to provide a divorce experience that breaks away from the conventional mold of lengthy, hostile and complex negotiations so that decisions related to things like the division of assets, living arrangements and child support are done so with your family wellbeing at the core.*

Can you see the difference? There's nothing in the Resolve Divorce example that talks about the names of court applications or legal practice areas. Instead, Resolve Divorce focus on their clients' problems and explain the solutions they want in a way they can relate to. Few clients want 'consent orders'. Instead, they want 'a property settlement with my ex' or, as Resolve puts it, a legal separation that will 'help you move forward in a positive and healthy way'.[1]

---

1   I spoke to Resolve Divorce's Managing Director Rose Cocchiaro on episode 46 of the Doing Law Differently podcast where she explained her approach as being about helping the overall wellbeing and personal growth of people and their families. Listen to the episode if you're interested to learn more.

Your clients aren't looking for a list of your skills and expertise. Nor do they want to buy time. In most cases, they don't even care how you achieve the result or who does the work to achieve it. What they want is recognition that you understand their problem, that you have a solution, and confidence that you will deliver it. What they care about is the *outcome*.

Law isn't unique here. You don't buy a hammer for the sake of owning one, but because it will help you to accomplish something. Maybe you want to hang a picture frame and the hammer will make your job of banging a nail into the wall much easier. Or perhaps you're putting together a shelf and a hammer will help knock the pieces together. Whatever the reason, the end result – the outcome – is more important than the hammer itself. The hammer is the solution to the problem. Any number of hammers would have got the job done.

But what if, when you walk past the sausage sizzle and into Bunnings on a Sunday morning, a salesperson greets you as you stare blankly at all the different varieties of hammers (who knew there could be so many types of hammers!) and asks what you're trying to achieve? Instead of telling you about the hammers, they focus on the problem you're trying to solve. What are you trying to get done? Maybe there's a better way of hanging the frame than with a hammer and nail. Maybe a drill and screw will be a better option? Perhaps a mallet is a better option than the hammer, helping you to knock the wood together without damaging it?

The point is, it's not about the tool, the hammer; what's more important is what you're trying to do with it. If you can help your clients achieve an outcome, rather than selling them a tool (like the use of your time), you have a much more attractive and relatable offer.

Hotels don't try to sell you a room and a bed for the night (the tools); instead, they sell the experience of relaxing and a good night's sleep (the outcome). Insurance companies don't sell insurance (the tool), they sell the peace of mind (the outcome). Luxury car companies don't sell metal, tyres and glass (the tools), they sell status (the outcome).

Resolve Divorce sell the outcome of 'a better settlement for you and your family ... without the negativity or emotional toll of traditional pathways'.

Stop promoting the *tools* you sell and instead start focusing on the *outcome*.

WHAT IS THE JOB TO BE DONE?

'Jobs to be done' is a theory that looks at why people engage a service provider or use a product. It's not about listing tasks and activities, but about understanding the real job that customers are trying to accomplish.

Harvard Business School professor Clayton Christensen explains it well:[2]

> *The fact that you're 18 to 35 years old with a college degree does not cause you to buy a product. It may be correlated with the decision, but it doesn't cause it. We developed this idea because we wanted to understand what causes us to buy a product, not what's correlated with it. We realized that the causal mechanism behind a purchase is, 'Oh, I've got a job to be done.' And it turns out that it's really effective in allowing a company to build products that people want to buy.*

Christensen shares an example about milkshakes that illustrates this point perfectly. McDonald's fast food chain was trying to increase

---

2   hbswk.hbs.edu/item/clay-christensens-milkshake-marketing. You can listen to Christensen tell the story himself in several interviews on YouTube, includingyoutube.com/watch?v=StcObeAxavY.

milkshake sales. They carried out research with milkshake buyers, asking how they should improve the drink by improving the characteristics of the ideal milkshake. McDonald's changed the milkshakes in response to the feedback, but they didn't see an increase in sales.

They then engaged Christensen's researchers to try a different approach. After watching milkshake buyers for many hours, they noticed that over half the milkshakes were sold before 8am, to people who were alone, who took the drinks away and drove in their car. They asked buyers questions like:

- 'What causes you to buy a milkshake?'

- 'Last time you were in the same situation and you didn't buy a milkshake, what did you buy?'

By asking these questions, the researchers discovered that the people who bought milkshakes had a long drive to work and the milkshake gave them something to do while they drove. They weren't hungry yet, but they knew they'd be hungry by 10am and the milkshake would do a good job of staving off hunger until then. Some of them had tried to purchase other products in the past, but a banana was eaten quickly and didn't entertain them for long enough; donuts were delicious, but they made buyers' hands sticky and left crumbs on their suit. A milkshake, on the other hand, took a while to drink, could sit in a cupholder and be held in one hand, and didn't make any mess. A milkshake does the job much better than any of its competitors.

Now that they understood the job to be done, McDonald's could take a different approach to increasing sales. Could they make their milkshakes thicker so they took longer to drink, or more interesting, with chunks of fruit? What other products could they add to their range that would hit the mark for a bored person with a long drive and only one hand?

'Jobs to be done' are solution agnostic. The focus isn't on what you have to sell, it's on understanding why people do what they do. When you shift to this perspective, you can start to recognise your client's needs before they even know they have them, and you can consider what services you can provide that your clients aren't yet asking for. What job causes your clients to hire you?

Again, we tend to think in terms of legal outcomes – they want a divorce or a property settlement. But is that what they *really* want? Do they want the court order, or do they want some certainty so they can move on with their life?

You might tell me you want to make your business run without you, but what you really want is to feel in control of your time. You want your business to serve you, not the other way around. You want to do things on *your* terms, instead of feeling like you're always working under pressure and to someone else's deadline. Chances are that if you were made completely redundant, you'd have no idea what to do with yourself!

When you reframe the question in this way, you'll quickly see that the solution you offer can be broader than a legal solution. Consider how you can help solve the whole problem, not just the legal part. For example, this could mean helping family law clients with emotional and financial counselling, or an employment lawyer helping employees with career counselling. Grevillea Law are estate planning specialists who don't just help clients to prepare a will, but also to create a keepsake for their families by helping them to write valuable messages to their children, spouse and other families in a purpose-designed journal, helping them to leave a legacy of love, as well as an inheritance.

Henry Ford's famous quote – 'If I had asked people what they wanted, they would have said faster horses' – illustrates this point perfectly. Don't fall into the trap of thinking your clients just want a faster horse.

If you do that, you won't think much beyond horses. But if you can forget about the horse and consider the job to be done, you might just go on to revolutionise your services.

WHAT MAKES YOU DIFFERENT AND REMARKABLE?

In 2010 we were the first business in Western Australia to offer conveyancing on a flat-fee pricing structure. Our price was the same regardless of the price of the property a client was buying or selling. This was unheard of, and gave us a unique point of difference from the hundreds of other lawyers and settlement agents offering conveyancing services. Add to that our targeted direct mail marketing campaign and the hundreds of positive client testimonials on our modern website and it was easy for potential clients to set us apart from our competitors.

One of your goals in business should be to create a point of difference that makes you memorable and unique. Do this well and you move into a league of your own and become incomparable with your competitors, making it easy for potential clients to choose you over others. It means you don't have to spend as much time chasing new work and you don't have to compete on price.

You'll come back to your point of difference when you start building your marketing campaigns, but it's a good idea to think about it now. What is going to make your offer different to everyone else's? This may develop as you bring your products to life, but you need to give it some thought before you dive in.

Traditional firms attempt to differentiate themselves by emphasising their history, market share, reputation, intellectual prowess of their people and high-profile clients. Compare these two statements taken from top-tier law firm websites.

Firm A

Operating as one global team, we use innovative systems and processes to ensure your work is delivered intelligently, efficiently and reliably. We care about the markets and communities we work within and constantly strive to make them better.

What does it all add up to? When you work with [firm name], you are partnering with a world-class and diverse team of client-focused professionals who can ensure you achieve your best results.

Firm B

Recognised as one of the world's most innovative law firms, [firm name] offers a different perspective to commercial thinking and the client experience. With access to a global platform, a team of over 2400 lawyers in 28 locations around the world works with clients to help them understand local challenges, navigate through regional complexity, and to find commercial solutions that deliver a competitive advantage for our clients.

Do you have any idea what these firms do? I don't.

Law firms that thrive in today's market are those whose point of difference is the value they provide to their clients. In other words, it's not about the firm, it's about their customers.

The examples above are a perfect fit for Seth Godin's 'boring slot':

> *In almost every market, the boring slot is filled. The product designed to appeal to the largest possible audience already exists, and displacing it is awfully difficult. Difficult because the very innocuousness of the market-leading product is its greatest asset. How can you market yourself as 'more bland than the*

leading brand'? The real growth comes with products that annoy,
offend, don't appeal, are too expensive, too cheap, too heavy, too
complicated, too simple – too something. (Of course, they're too too
for some people, but just perfect for others.)[3]

According to Tim Williams, your brand shouldn't just be different, it should be remarkable: 'A middle-of-the-road, standing-for-everything positioning strategy is unlikely to get you there.'[4]

HOW CAN YOU DIFFERENTIATE YOURSELF?

Here are six ideas to get you thinking about how you can differentiate your business beyond experience and reputation.

Do pricing differently

How can your pricing model set you apart?

Having charged fixed prices for so long, it's easy for me to fall into the trap of thinking that fixed fee is the norm, but it's far from it. It's still more common for lawyers to charge on a timed basis than to quote a fixed price. So even though you might not see fixed pricing as something that differentiates your service, it does.

Don't just tell people that you charge fixed fees, show them. Go that extra step and publish your prices on your website.

We advertise fixed prices for all our flagship products (more on that in the next chapter). This is so uncommon in the legal profession that it instantly sets us apart. Lawyers are reluctant to publish prices, but most other businesses do it. Would you buy a jacket, book a flight or

---

3   *Purple Cow: Transform your business by being remarkable*, Seth Godin, p92.
4   *Positioning for Professionals*, Tim Williams, p26.

hire a car without knowing the price? If not, why expect people to buy your legal services without knowing what they'll cost?

Deliver an exceptional customer experience

Being competent and delivering on time are the bare basics. To provide excellent service you need to do much more than deliver the basics. When it comes to customer experience, where else to draw inspiration from than the Happiest Place on Earth. Disney is regularly recognised for its magical and personalised approach to customer experience. Every guest is treated as a VIP, and staff go over and above to ensure that guests want to come back.

How can you create some magic in your firm?

Brisbane Family Law Centre strive to deliver an exceptional customer experience that's unlike that of any other law firm. Their offices are decorated with bright, patterned wallpaper and neon lights, their advices are delivered using colourful infographics, not long letters, and they send handwritten birthday cards to every client the firm has ever had.[5]

Excel at quality of work, speed of delivery or convenience

Can you demonstrate that you produce work of a higher standard? Maybe you have a high success rate with the type of work you do that sets you apart from others?

Our point of difference with our probate application services is the on-the-spot application – the application prepared before your eyes during your meeting with one of our lawyers. What typically takes

---

5   Learn more about BFLC in my interview with founder Clarissa Rayward in episode 59 of the Doing Law Differently podcast.

weeks and several appointments with a traditional law firm is completed in under an hour.

Create a unique methodology

Most clients are looking for a solution to a problem. They're interested in an outcome or result. How you get there is up to you. Stand out by creating a unique methodology for handling matters. Owning a process makes it easier to pitch and differentiate your service.

Aptum Legal are an example, having developed a unique project management approach that sets them apart. Their methodology addresses the shortcomings experienced by clients in litigation matters and enables them to clearly set themselves apart from their competitors.[6]

Find your tilt

In *Content Inc*, Joe Pulizzi describes differentiation in relation to content as 'content tilting'. He explains: 'Without "tilting" your content just enough to truly have a different story to tell, your content will fade into the rest of the clutter and be forgotten.'

What unique stance or perspective can you take on your service?

Shelby Timmins (Divorce Done Differently) and Anne-Marie Cade (Divorce Right) are both lawyers turned Divorce Coaches who offer a completely different tilt on their services. Shelby acknowledges and embraces the fact that at the heart of every divorce is a family that's hurting. She believes it's time for lawyers to take a step back from divorce and for a new kind of team – composed of sensitive, trained, multi-disciplinary professionals – to take the reins and to take

---

6   Listen to episode 3 of the Doing Law Differently podcast to hear from Aptum's Director Nigel Evans.

a holistic approach that recognises that the divorce process should be more about relationships and emotion that legal process.

Anne-Marie takes a different tilt, encouraging her clients to see divorce as a business transaction and to use her service to support them to set themselves up for the next part of their life; for example, by teaching them how to understand and manage personal finances.[7]

Find your niche market

If you narrow your focus to a niche or even a micro-niche, you can position yourself as the obvious go-to expert for anyone who fits that market.

Sarah Jefford is an Australian Surrogacy Lawyer whose only practice area is family creation law. She has written a book about surrogacy law, hosts the Australian Surrogacy Law podcast, and has also been an IVF mum, an egg donor and a surrogate, so she offers a unique perspective on her clients' problems.

---

7 Both Shelby and Anne-Marie have been guests on the Doing Law Differently podcast. Listen to episodes 49 (Shelby) and 55 (Anne-Marie) for a deeper insight into these different tilts.

KEY POINTS IN THIS CHAPTER

1. When it comes to your services, it's not about you, it's about your clients. Forget describing your qualifications; how do you solve your client's problem?

2. Think beyond legal outcomes to consider what your clients *really* want to achieve.

3. Your business won't stand out by fitting in. What's your point of difference? What makes you remarkable?

 ## IT'S TIME TO DO LAW DIFFERENTLY

- Broaden your thinking from what legal services you can provide to how you can solve your clients' problems.

- What is your client's job to be done?

- What makes you different and remarkable?

Step 4:
Productise your services

'Product excellence is now paramount to business success –
not control of information, not a stranglehold on distribution,
not overwhelming marketing power.'

Eric Schmidt, *How Google Works*

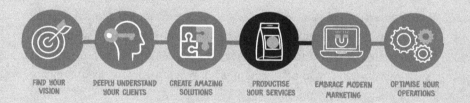

FIND YOUR
VISION

DEEPLY UNDERSTAND
YOUR CLIENTS

CREATE AMAZING
SOLUTIONS

PRODUCTISE
YOUR SERVICES

EMBRACE MODERN
MARKETING

OPTIMISE YOUR
OPERATIONS

In step two you worked out who your clients are and in step three you thought about how you can solve their problems. Step four is the heart of the Productise and Profit method and is all about how to package, price and deliver your services.

Selling products makes it easier to:

- attract prospects – you offer tangible solutions, not a list of skills and capabilities

- convert them to clients – the solution you offer stands out from your competitors for all the right reasons – you're the credible expert offering a solution to your client's problem at a transparent price

- deliver an outstanding service – your system for delivery will enhance your customer experience. Your focus is on delivering an outcome in the most effective way.

When you productise your services, you save time and reduce dependency on you preparing customised scopes for every client who walks through the door. You make it easier for your staff to sell your services as they know what you offer and at what price, and you make it easier for clients to buy from you.

The aim is to create a product ecosystem where each product works in harmony with the others. Together, the products maximise value and increase demand. By creating an ecosystem you will remain relevant in your client's journey and meet their evolving needs.

THE PERILS OF THE BILLABLE HOUR

Before we start talking about products, now seems a good time to give you a stern talking to about the lawyers' old friend, the billable hour.

You know how this works. Client engages lawyer for legal advice. Lawyer gives client an abstract hourly rate and proceeds to record the time they spend on the matter in six-minute units. At the end of the month, lawyer sends a bill to the client, who has no idea what number to expect at the bottom of it and no real way of working out whether they've received value for money.

Criticisms about the billable hour are among the most common complaints we hear about the legal profession. They're the core of many a lawyer joke, and unsurprisingly so. The billable hour has served partners well, many of whom have made a decent profit from what others have described as a pyramid scheme. For everyone else, though, clients and employees alike, the billable hour is fraught.

Let's unpack why.

The billable hour doesn't serve the client's interests

The billable hour prevents law firms from being aligned to client interests, and because you've read this far, you know the importance of aligning a firm to its clients' interests. Remember, clients don't care about time, they care about outcomes.

Billable hours ignore whether work actually furthers the client's interests. Is an hour spent formatting a document worth the same as the hour spent drafting it? Most clients have little concept of how long it takes to draft an agreement, research a legal issue or prepare for court, and many have no capacity to check whether the services they were charged for were necessary. What's more, the quality of output doesn't necessarily correlate to the time put in. A junior lawyer might take two hours to complete a task that would take a senior practitioner 30 minutes.

So for a start, billable hours provide little or no predictability about cost. A client doesn't know how much a service will cost until after the fact.

The billable hour rewards inefficiency

The billable hour penalises what most other businesses reward: efficiency and productivity. In firms that charge for time, a staff member who gets work done efficiently is penalised by having to do more work to meet their billable targets. When individual performance is based on how much time is spent, there will be a temptation to spend as much time as possible on any given task.

The focus is on inputs, not outcomes. But if technology can help a lawyer to achieve a job in 10 minutes instead of one hour, shouldn't they use that technology?

The billable hour can cause ill health

The billable hour is the key measure of performance for most lawyers. This leads to the pressure to work long hours, skimping on sleep, missing family events and rarely switching off. It's common knowledge that long working hours and heavy workloads increase the likelihood of mental illness. The *2019 Meritas Australia & New Zealand Wellness Survey* revealed that of the lawyers surveyed:

- 68% had experienced depression or knew someone close to them in the workplace who had

- 85% had experienced anxiety or knew someone close to them in the workplace who had.[1]

---

1   swaab.com.au/assets/download/Meritas-Wellness-Survey-Report.pdf

At least half of all respondents believed there is more than a 50% chance that someone close to them would experience depression or anxiety during their career (50% and 64% respectively).

Wellness is becoming a hot topic in law firms, with the introduction of plenty of initiatives that aim to raise awareness of and combat mental health and wellbeing issues. A study on the use and effectiveness of wellbeing initiatives implemented by a large Australian public sector legal service organisation found that although there is much more awareness of these initiatives, they are only accessed by a small proportion of people. One of the key reasons for not accessing initiatives was 'heavy workload and a lack of available time' and the resulting 'need to catch up on work that had not been completed during the time out'.[2]

There are only 24 hours in a day

If you're charging for your time, you're only making money while you're working. Sure, you can hire more people and charge for their hours, but the amount you can make is still limited by time × people × billable hour.

I won't lie: changing the way you charge for services isn't as simple as just putting a price tag on a service. It is a whole business model change, but it's one that's essential if you want to build a business that can run without you. After all, if you're charging for your personal time, you can only make money while you're working.

What I know for certain is that if you want to start living the lifestyle you desire, you need to untie your revenue from the exertion of your time.

---

2   unswlawjournal.unsw.edu.au/wp-content/uploads/2018/05/Poynton-et-al.pdf.

SO WHAT ARE 'PRODUCTISED LEGAL SERVICES'?

When I think of the term 'product', what comes to mind is a super-market aisle packed full of goods: bottles, packages and labels. You might imagine a factory production line and think of commodities like toilet paper, cereal boxes or chocolate bars.

Chances are, you don't think of legal services.

Legal services aren't something that you'll find on a supermarket shelf (at least not yet!), but they can be sold as products nonetheless. Legal products can:

1. be something *tangible*, like a contract, a letter of demand or an online course

2. involve the *provision of services*, such as advice or representation.

This second category is a 'productised service'. These are services that are packaged and sold like a typical product, such as a box of cake mix. They offer the *convenience of a product* and the *personalisation of a service*. They're a solution to a client's problem. Everything your client needs is pre-packaged safely inside.

Consider the box of cake mix. It might have:

- *on the front:* a catchy name and picture

- *on the back:* the recipe, which is the ingredients and method for making the cake

- *on the left side:* serving size and nutritional value

- *on the right side:* company information, testimonials, contact information

- *on the back:* the price.

A productised legal service also has:

- *a catchy name and description of the outcome* – perhaps a logo or picture
- what the service *includes* (ingredients) and a predefined *process* to deliver the service (method)
- *a fixed scope* (serving size) and *defined benefits* (nutrition)
- *testimonials* and *contact information*
- a *fixed price*.[3]

Like a box of cake mix, productised legal services make it easy to see what's on offer. Buyers know the desired outcome (are they buying chocolate cake or carrot cake?), exactly what is included and what the price will be.

We often speak of 'unbundling' legal services (the reduction of full-service retainers into discrete parts and limited-scope retainers). Productised legal services is 'packaging up' legal services. Unlike bespoke engagements where each retainer is prepared on a per-matter basis, products are a standard service. They include a routine set of tasks, outcomes, and a standard, fixed price. In this way, a legal service product is no different to any other product.

Products help you to simplify your business. They let you 'work hard once' and leverage that hard work time and time again. They enable you to come up with the recipe and then let others make the cake.

You might be thinking, 'Every engagement is unique, I can't standardise it', or perhaps, 'I can't possibly anticipate every need my clients might have and create a product for it'. I'd challenge you on the first; yes, every engagement *is* unique, but most can still be standardised to at least some degree. However, the point is not to create a product

---

3   Adapted from britewrx.com/blog/why-you-need-to-productize-your-services-and-how-it-works.

for every possible problem you may need to solve (we tried that – it failed), but instead to create a 'product ecosystem' that consists of:

- **Flagship products.** Your flagship products come with a predetermined scope, a fixed price, and have a system for delivery. They offer entry points to your business and form the basis of your business's brand. They are what attract new business, position you in the market and let you systemise your work.

- **Bespoke engagements.** Your bespoke engagements will have a customised scope, a fixed price based on the value provided to that specific client, and – because they are bespoke in nature – don't have a predetermined system for delivery.

Let me explain how this all works.

HOW DO PRODUCTISED LEGAL SERVICES WORK?

You're used to buying products, so it's probably not too much of a stretch to imagine creating a tangible legal product, giving it a price tag and selling it.

Where you may be confused is with the 'service' aspect. So, how do productised legal services work? They have three essential elements:

1. a predefined scope

2. a fixed price

3. a system or method for delivery.

Understanding how to create productised legal services is crucial to implementing the Productise and Profit method, so let's have a look at each of these three in detail.

The three essential elements of productised legal services

1. You must have a predefined scope

Just as a box of cake mix has pre-prepared ingredients to make a certain cake, a productised service has a predefined, standard scope that will deliver a certain outcome.

Imagine buying your favourite cake mix. Maybe, like me, it's White Wings Double Chocolate Fudge Brownie Mix, or perhaps you're more of a Betty Crocker Vanilla Cake Mix fan. Either way, when you pick up that box, you're buying the standardised recipe that has been written and mass-produced in hundreds of thousands of blue (or red) cake mix boxes. You're not getting a custom-written recipe designed just to your liking with your favourite icing and sprinkles on a $4 cake mix range. It's a standard product.

Similarly, the scope of a productised service is pre-prepared to achieve a standard outcome, not custom-designed to suit the unique needs of every person who walks through the door.

Residential builders do this well. Most offer a series of pre-designed house plans that you can choose from. They come at a fixed price with a standard set of finishes. You can customise the colour of your walls, type of carpet and choice of tiles in the kitchen, but add another bedroom or increase the size of the bathroom and you're into bespoke territory.

Productised services work in the same way. They offer a standard scope of services designed to solve a specific problem for a specific type of client. There may be some add-ons, but the hard work of designing the scope is done once by you and presented as a solution many times over.

When you offer a productised service, you go from saying, 'here are all my skills and expertise, how can I help you?' to saying, 'here is the solution to your problem'.

The traditional law model is based on the assumption that lawyers will provide a 'full service' to each client. In other words, they will handle *every aspect* of a matter in its entirety, from legal advice and strategy to document preparation and everything in between.

Productised services, on the other hand, are about *clearly defining a limited scope of services* and selling them as a package. The scope must be clearly detailed upfront and should:

- define the parameters of the service
- detail any milestones and deliverables
- specify what is *excluded* from the service.

Most mechanics won't touch your car unless there's a pre-authorised scope of works. As soon as they open the bonnet and discover you've got an unexpected leak, they pick up the phone and start to negotiate a new scope.

I like to think of legal services as on a spectrum. On one side is self-represented or DIY, and on the other side is full-service or done-for-you.

Your job is to work out where a particular product lies on the spectrum and determine what work you'll complete and what you will leave with the client. This forms the basis of your written scope.

Start by mapping out the service. Look at each step and ask yourself what work you will complete and what is outside the scope. The scope we use for our application for Probate On The Spot service looks something like this:

We will:

- prepare your application based on the information you provide in our checklist

- prepare a consent notice for any non-applying executor

- send you the application to review

- arrange for you to sign the affidavit and file your application at the court.

This service does not include:

- making enquiries to verify the estate's assets and liabilities

- preparing an application to prove an informal will or codicil or a copy of a will or codicil

- preparing any evidence relating to the due execution of the will or codicil.

As you can see, this product is for a straightforward application. If the client doesn't have the original will, we'll re-scope and re-quote. Then we're into bespoke territory – more on that later.

Managing fixed-scope work

Here are three tips for fixed-scope work:

- **A robust costs agreement is essential.** A detailed, written costs agreement with a carefully drafted scope is essential. The lawyer drafting the agreement must have a good understanding of the legal issues to be dealt with and tasks to be undertaken in the matter.

  As well as setting out the scope of works, it may be necessary to include advice about any risks to the client presented by the limited scope.

  For example, when preparing a will, often a client doesn't want to instruct us to prepare a binding death benefit nomination, taking the view that they'll do it themselves. In this case, it's prudent for our scope of services to clearly set out that we've advised them of the risks of not engaging us to complete that work; for example, that the superannuation may not be paid in accordance with their wishes.

- **The fixed-price scope.** Like most things in law, managing a fixed-price scope is a skill that comes with practice. You need to have a good understanding of the scope of services so you can make sure you act within the scope and can give a new quote where necessary.

  The best way to manage this is to be as upfront as possible. As soon as your client hints at engaging you for work that is outside the scope, tell them that it's not included in their quoted fee. If you start to complete additional work without making it clear that the services will be charged in addition to the quoted price, it makes it much more difficult to charge more later. Instead, prepare a new scope and price at the earliest opportunity.

- **The staged scope.** For longer or more complex engagements, a staged scope is a useful mechanism to define the stages of work and ensure that both you and your client recognise when work is complete. Stages of work should be aligned to the fee structure, so it's clear what proportion of the quote will be billed at what stage.

Resolution Family Law is our family law brand. Our flagship product is a fixed-price application for consent orders. The service is for separating couples who have already agreed on the terms of their property and parenting settlement and simply need the agreement to be formalised. As it turns out, in family law, an agreement is one thing until it is put into writing. Then it may be something completely different, and what our client thought was agreed often turns out to be disputed.

When we recognised the common theme, we changed the way we billed the service to make sure we weren't losing out when the client wanted to change the terms of our engagement to include mediation or negotiation services, instead of just formalising an agreement.

We split the cost of the service into two stages – preparing the application and arranging signing. The price is front-loaded, since that's where the majority of our work takes place. If the agreement isn't signed, we simply bill stage one and prepare a new scope to cover the services the client now needs.

2. You must have fixed pricing

Just as your cake mix has a price label on the supermarket shelf, a productised service has a fixed price. Because your service has a pre-defined scope you can price it in advance.

Imagine going to a supermarket where the aisles and products have no price tags. You have no idea what you'll be charged for your shopping until you've taken it home and consumed it, at which time you're sent a bill for the products you've consumed. Sounds crazy, doesn't it?

Setting a price for your product involves finding a win–win between the client's perceived value of the service and your cost of delivery and profit margins. Measuring the value the client receives isn't easy. In fact, the value will be different for every client.

There are three types of fixed-pricing models to consider for your legal services:

• menu pricing

• value pricing

• subscription pricing.

In short, menu pricing is about pricing a service, value pricing is about pricing the client, and a subscription model provides a fixed fee on a recurring basis.

I recently presented to a group of lawyers about different pricing methods and used a debt collection example to demonstrate the different pricing options.

The entry point for debt collection is usually a letter demanding payment of the debt.

Firm A advertises a menu price for letters of demand at $295 per letter, regardless of the size of the debt.

Firm B has implemented value pricing, so before giving you a quote, they talk to you to get a better understanding of the circumstances:

- What is the size of the debt? A $5 million debt is going to be worth more to you than a $5000 debt.

- What is the debtor's attitude to repaying the debt?

- How important is it to your business that the debt be repaid? Are you about to go under, or are you demanding debt more on the principal of the matter?

After speaking to you, Firm B sends a quote for $1000.

Firm C has a subscription service; $500 per month for unlimited demand letters and other debt collection advice.

So, you can see that the different models produce different costs for the same product.

Menu pricing works well for commodity work that is competitive and is a good way to attract new clients to a firm. Value pricing works well for more complex matters with unique components. Subscription models are great for bringing ongoing revenue and can have a lower barrier to entry because of the smaller upfront cost to the client.

Below we'll explore each pricing method in more detail, but it's important to understand that this brief discussion does not do justice to all there is to know about pricing. Pricing is one of the most significant functions in a business, and you shouldn't underestimate it, nor should it be an afterthought.[4]

---

4   If you're interested to learn more about pricing, listen to episode 38 of the Doing Law Differently podcast, where I talk all things pricing with pricing expert John Chisholm.

Menu pricing

Menu pricing is just as it sounds – a fixed price for a specific service determined by the seller, independently of any buyer.

Most people start their journey with menu pricing by working out how much time something will take them and then charging the hourly rate equivalent. This is really just time billing by another name, but if this is what it takes to help you get started with productising your services, I say go for it.

When I talk about menu pricing, though, I mean charging one price for a standard set of services. It's fixed in two ways: not only do you charge the same amount for each service, but you also charge the same amount to every client.

Some things to consider when determining the price of your product include:

- What is the cost of production? Include rent, wages, software costs, office supplies, marketing.

- What is the risk to the firm?

- How does the client benefit from the product? Is it increased wealth? Reduced risk? Time saving? Decreased liability?

- What is the market rate for a similar service?

- What is the likelihood of receiving more work from the client?

- Does the work involve a learning opportunity for staff?

Beware of pricing your services too low. Not only will you miss out on revenue, you may also deter clients who fear your service must be too good to be true. This was one of the biggest challenges we faced when we launched Flat Rate Settlements. We were the first in Western Australia to adopt a fixed, flat fee for conveyancing. Almost every prospective client would ask us 'what's the catch?' or 'are there any hidden fees?' They simply thought that our offer was too good to be true. We put a lot of effort into convincing prospective clients that we were legitimate, including publishing hundreds of client testimonials on our website and making sure new business enquiries were answered promptly by experienced staff.

Another example is our Probate On The Spot product. This product is an application for probate prepared 'on the spot' during a client consultation. We use custom-designed software to automate the collection of data, open the file and generate the application and other documents. When we launched the service it was delivered by law clerks under the supervision of lawyers and could be completed in about 45 minutes. As amateur fixed pricers, we charged a price that was equal to the time we spent. Since launching, we have increased the price by more than 250% and our number of new files has remained consistent.

This was an interesting experiment in pricing that taught us:

- Price should not be based solely on the cost of production. Doing so probably means we're missing out on income.

- Not all clients are looking for the cheapest price and, in fact, we don't really want to act for those who attach a very low value to the service.

- We are prone to undervaluing our own work and need to be aware of this when pricing.

- When we charged a higher fee, our staff felt more pride in their work and our clients were more interested in and prepared for the process.

- When we increased our prices, we attracted more clients who were willing to engage us for estate administration services too. In other words, the average fee per client went up, not just on account of the product fee increase, but because they engaged us for other work.

- The value of the service is, in part, our effectiveness in delivery – the entire process completed in one convenient consultation. We should charge a premium for this, not a discounted rate.

Remember, clients are paying for outcomes. While efficient processes and productisation will undoubtedly lower your costs of production, you don't need to pass that saving on to your clients in full. Your efficiency and effectiveness doesn't reduce your service's value to your clients, it increases it. Undervaluing your services not only means you leave money on the table; it may also mean that potential clients don't engage you for fear that there's a hidden catch.

The Probate On The Spot example also addresses one of the most common fears I hear about fixed pricing – 'what if I get the price wrong?' Pricing legal services isn't easy. I always say it's more art than science, but fortunately your price doesn't have to be set in stone. You can adjust your price after you've received feedback from your market. Your price is simply a number on a website or brochure – it is easy to change.

Value pricing

The second type of fixed pricing for your productised services is value pricing.

Value pricing is about pricing the outcome or worth to the client, not about pricing the deliverables that make up the service. The price you charge for a service will vary for each client depending on a number of factors, including complexity, service delivery method, time pressure and the value they receive from it. You still charge a fixed amount, but there is much more variability because you set a price for each client, not for the product.

Value pricing is based on the subjective theory of value, a belief that products and services are only valuable insofar as there is a buyer who desires them. 'Value', then, is as perceived by the customer, not by the internal costs incurred in generating a service.

The more you speak to your clients and understand their objectives, fears, goals and priorities, the more you'll realise that value *is* subjective.

Ronald Baker, author and founder of pricing thinktank VeraSage Institute, talks about the distinction between the cost, price and value of water.[5]

He explains that the cost to produce a bottle of water will be different to the price you pay, which itself will vary depending where you buy it. If you buy a bottle of water in a shop you might pay $2.00, at a sports game it will cost more, and more still if you bought it from a mini-bar. That price has little to do with the cost of the water.

The value is another component altogether.

If you're in the desert and haven't had water for four days, it is priceless, but that same quantity of water is worth a lot less when you want it to wash the dog. Or imagine if your house got flooded. Now water has a negative value because you have to pay somebody to pump it out.

Why is this the case? Because value is subjective.

Think back to the debt collection example I shared earlier. One indicator of value is the size of the debt – the collection of a $5 million debt is worth more to you than a $5000 debt. The size of the debt is just one factor, though. What about the importance to your business of the debt being paid? Are you fighting it on principle, or is your

---

5   Listen to Ron share this analogy in this excellent presentation: youtube.com/watch?v=fPL5YnDXaYE.

business about to go under but receiving payment of this debt will be enough to save you. That's a whole lot more valuable.

'Client value' is the perception of what a product or service is worth to a customer versus the possible alternatives. It can be broken down to a simple equation: Client value = Benefits − Cost.

Cost is much bigger than price. When a client buys a product or service they don't just spend money on it, they also invest time, effort, convenience and energy.

Likewise, the benefits can be more than the outcome that the product is designed to achieve. Benefits can include brand affiliation, experience, knowledge, personal development and access to a solution.

Each client will place different levels of importance on each cost and benefit.

Ronald Baker is an expert on value pricing in professional service firms, and if you're considering implementing value pricing in your business you should read his book *Implementing Value Pricing*. In the book, Baker sets out eight steps to implementing value pricing:

1. Have a conversation with your customer to determine their needs and wants, the scope of work and communicate the value you can add.

2. Present the information from step one to a value council, whose purpose is to set a price for the customer, not the service. The value council should establish three levels of service – think American Express Green, Gold, Platinum and Black cards.

3. Don't offer a single take-it-or-leave-it price. Instead, offer three different pricing options.

4. Present the pricing options to the customer.

5. Codify the option selected by the customer in a Fixed Price Agreement (scope of works).

6. Project manage the scope of work. Detail who will complete work and when it will be delivered.

7. Proactively manage scope creep and change orders.

8. Complete After Action Reviews to assess the pricing of each major engagement.

Lynn & Brown Lawyers are a boutique law firm based in Morley, Western Australia. The firm practises in family law, litigation and dispute resolution, and commercial law, and operate entirely on a value billing model, following Baker's eight steps. For every engagement they prepare a quote that includes three tiers of service options for the client to choose from. Those prices are set by a pricing council who are responsible for pricing the firm's work. Director Steven Brown says that the firm is more profitable now than they were when they sold time and have much more enjoyment in the way they practice law.[6]

Subscription pricing

The third type of fixed pricing for your productised services is subscription pricing.

When I think about subscriptions, the first thing that comes to mind for me is magazine subscriptions. These days, though, subscription pricing is everywhere. We used to hire DVDs on a Friday night, now we subscribe to Netflix for on-demand streaming. We used to buy singles or albums, first in CD format, then on a pay-per download; now we subscribe to Spotify for on-demand music streaming. We subscribe to Amazon Prime for free shipping, HelloFresh for dinner delivered to

---

6   Steven Brown spoke to me about his firm's transition to value pricing on episode 17 of the Doing Law Differently podcast.

our door, and Dropbox for online document storage. Even luxury car brand Porsche have a subscription model to attract younger drivers to the company.

The subscription economy is one of the most transformative innovations of the modern age. Businesses such as Netflix, Uber and Spotify succeed because they have tapped into a new era that's becoming known as 'the end of ownership'. They have asked what their customers want and have designed services that give them that. As customers, we increasingly value access and outcomes over ownership. We want the benefits that products will bring without the burden of maintenance and upkeep. Netflix gives us on-demand access to an entire movie store without the burden of driving to the store, checking if our film is in stock, hoping the disc isn't scratched when we get home, and, of course, eliminates those hefty late fees. Spotify does the same for music. Why own hundreds of CDs or spend hours waiting for music files to download, when Spotify gives you instant access to the world's music on any device?

Clients are used to buying subscriptions in other areas of their lives, so it's logical that we're starting to see these models crop up in the legal space too.

Put simply, subscription pricing is where a product or service is made available for a fixed price on a recurring basis. Subscriptions are about *access* to services, not for specific deliverables.

Robbie Kellman Baxter, author of *The Forever Transaction*, describes this trend as The Membership Economy and says:

> It means moving away from an ownership model to one of access, from a single payment to multiple recurring payments, from an anonymous transaction to a known relationship, and from one-way — or even two-way — communication to a full community fathered under the umbrella of the organisation.

Her book also offers a how-to guide for building a subscription model.

The most common use of subscription models in the legal profession is lawyers offering outsourced in-house counsel services.

Law Squared offer a subscription service known as Law Squared as a Service (LSaaS) for business and corporate clients as an alternative to, or extension to, an in-house legal team. LSaaS leverages Law Squared's four legal teams of commercial, corporate, employment and litigation to offer a complete outsourced legal function at a fixed monthly cost.

Proximity is a professional services organisation providing legal, commercial and governance advisory solutions. They offer a variety of different pricing models, including subscription pricing, which enables their clients to access to ongoing, proactive legal services.

3. You must have a system for delivery

The third element of a productised service is systemised delivery.

Think back to your box of cake mix and picture the method that tells you what to do with the ingredients and in what order.

Likewise, a productised service should have a method for delivery. A process for service delivery is the engine of productised services and are what truly distinguishes a productised service from a typical fixed-price service.

Systems only work for a standard service. If you offer a custom scope to every client, your process will look different for every engagement. With productised services, you follow the same process every time. Each time you deliver a service you can make improvements to your systems and benefit time and time again.

With good systems you will increase the standard and quality of your work and at the same time reduce the time it takes to deliver the service. Better still, you can automate the grunt work, freeing your time to work on the things you enjoy most.

Streamlined and effective processes are integral to a product's success. The aim is twofold. First, to solve your client's problem while providing an exceptional client experience. Second, to standardise production to reduce cost, minimise risk and improve performance. The key is to find the right balance between the two.

My love for standardised processes began shortly after we introduced our flat-rate pricing structure for real estate conveyancing. My workload was increasing and the work was high pressure and time sensitive. To make things worse, I was the only team member in the conveyancing department and I only worked part time. I needed a way to organise my work so I didn't have to rely on my brain to remember where each file was at and to make sure nothing was missed. I worked with our software developer to design process models – a file level workflow that dictates the tasks required to complete each stage (milestone) of a matter. Within each milestone is a group of tasks required to complete the milestone. These tasks are much more than a static task list. They:

- only appear in a team member's task list on the day they should be commenced

- pre-select the relevant document template that automatically attaches any relevant documents

- delegate to the most appropriate person on the team

- pre-populate due dates and priorities

- assess and respond to conditions on the file to determine whether they even need to be created at all; I don't want a task to tell me to chase a finance approval that is already on the file.

These process models have revolutionised our service delivery. They mean we can rely on the systems to keep our files in order and on track. We can see at a glance which step of the process every file is at and other staff can easily pick up a file in the file manager's absence. Having system for delivery means we can hire law students and other professionals to deliver our services – all they need to do is follow the process.

We went on to design systems for delivering all our firm's flagship productised services, each time creating more intelligent and effective processes that transformed the way we do business and the value we create for our clients.

The service blueprint map

One of the most useful tools I have found for developing systems is the service blueprint map. A service blueprint is an extension of a customer journey map that helps you to visualise the relationship between different service components from a client's perspective. As well as identifying the interactions a client has with a service, the blueprint goes deeper to look at the businesses actions and processes that support those interactions. The two together are how you design an exceptional system for delivery. The result is a complete picture of how a service is delivered – end to end and surface to core.

On the following page is an example of a service blueprint map.

Service blueprint (example)

	Google Ads SEO listing	Website		Online enquiry form	Email	Checklist	Office building Reception Consultation Room		Bill
Physical evidence									
Customer actions	Researches problem	Visits website	Telephone to ask questions	Book appointment online	Receive email confirmation	Complete checklist for appointment	Attend office for appointment		Pay bill
LINE OF INTERACTION									
Frontstage actions			Answer phone call, provide answers and information				Reception welcome	Give advice at consultation	
LINE OF VISIBILITY									
Backstage actions	Write and publish content/ Google Ad			Maintain calendars		Create and send checklist		Years of education and training!	
LINE OF INTERNAL INTERACTION									
Supporting processes		Website maintenance and analytics	Telephone call hunt groups	Online booking form system	Email confirmation				Billing and accounting system

The service blueprint map is discussed further below.

UNDERSTANDING THE ESSENTIAL COMPONENTS OF A SERVICE BLUEPRINT MAP

Service designers use the metaphor of a stage to help explain the essential concepts of service design. Service components are broken down into frontstage and backstage, depending on whether the customer sees them or not.

The front stage is everything the client sees – their interactions with you, your booking system, correspondence and end products. Backstage processes are those that are required to deliver the product, but that the client doesn't see.

Think of a theatre performance. The audience sees everything on the stage, but there is a whole ecosystem behind the stage that is working to bring the performance to life. What goes on backstage is just as important in bringing the show to life, and has as much of an impact on the audience's experience as the show itself.

The line of visibility is the barrier between what customers can and can't see. You can think of this like the background set on a stage.

The horizontal rows in the blueprint are known as swim lanes and vertical columns relate to a point in time.

Service blueprinting should be carried out as a team with as many stakeholder representatives as possible. When you build the blueprint, it's important to create it based on real customer and employee accounts. In other words, map what people *actually* do, not what best practice says they should do, or what you'd like them to do. How things are supposed to be done isn't always how they are done. By starting with the current state, you can get a proper understanding of what is really happening and then work out how to improve it.

In practical terms, get your team together, grab a bunch of post-it notes and pens, and find a big wall. Then get started with mapping the blueprint swim lanes:

- **Customer journey** – start here. Map each of the elements of the customer journey. These are the things the customer does to interact with your service.

- **Employee frontstage and backstage actions** – start with the frontstage actions. These are the things your staff do that your customer sees; for example, a telephone call or meeting. Then move down to add the corresponding backstage actions. These are the things your staff do that your customers don't see. They might include the preparation for a conference or preparing an affidavit.

- **Map support processes** – support processes are the people and resources that are required to deliver the service, but that the customer doesn't see. Your clerk filing documents at the court, the assistant who types your dictation and the website form that collects important data.

- **Map evidence** – evidence is the tangible elements associated with the delivery of a service. A letter of advice, a brochure or an affidavit are examples of evidence.

From there, you can use the service blueprint to identify any pain points and moments that matter and set about improving them. The blueprint will also help you identify the processes and resources you need to create your systemised delivery.

HOW TO IDENTIFY YOUR FLAGSHIP PRODUCTS

Your flagship products are your predefined, advertised productised services. They form the core of your business's brand. They address a core need but also act as a gateway to your bespoke services.

It's a good idea to create a 'lowest common denominator' flagship product with a scope that covers the most common scenario for each service.

Consider what parts of your service could be packaged and productised, or whether the entire process should become a product in itself. Your product needs to solve your client's problem, so scope is important. Too narrow and your product won't be meaningful, too wide and you might miss the mark in terms of your clients' needs, or your price point might be too high.

Entry point work often makes for good flagship services. What are the questions that your clients are asking at the start of their legal problem, or even before their legal problem arises? What is their first touchpoint with the legal system? If you can provide a product that targets this need you can build a relationship with the client right from the beginning of their journey and become the obvious choice when they need more legal help.

Many lawyers shy away from entry level legal services in chase of prestigious or high-profile matters, but in doing so they miss out on valuable opportunities.

Entry or routine legal work often lends itself well to process-driven delivery and is perfect for productising. It's this type of work that is increasingly being offered by alternative legal service providers who are harnessing technology to provide low-cost, high-value services. LegalZoom is a prime example of this, providing tools and templates to assist consumers with do-it-yourself legal services.

While alternative providers might have technology on side, many lack the skill, and knowledge held by legal practitioners who are experienced in providing these services. If you can harness your legal know-how effectively, you have a huge competitive advantage in productising your services.

After you've productised an entry-point service, you can start to consider what comes next on your client's journey and you'll be well on your way to building your product ecosystem.

One of our flagship products is a letter of demand for payment of a debt. We charge a small fee and the product is delivered by an entirely automated process (well, almost; we haven't automated posting the letter in the mailbox just yet). The letter is the entry point to many other services. As it turns out, many clients who send demand letters need legal representation to obtain or enforce a judgement, and others need credit management advice or terms and conditions of trade.

Routine and recurring services generally have predictable outcomes, making them prime candidates for productisation. Drafting an employment contract is a good example of a recurring engagement. Your client needs a new one each time they hire a new staff member, and the process and outcome are routine and predictable.

FIRST TEST YOUR SOLUTION AS A MINIMUM VIABLE PRODUCT

The goal of testing your solution as a minimum viable product (MVP) is to maximise learning while minimising risk, effort and investment. The idea is to understand your client's interest in your service without fully developing it.

An MVP isn't about offering less functionality or a poor-quality service. It's about doing the least amount of work to get the most valuable feedback from having your product in the market. It's important to get the balance right, though. Cut out too many features and you'll end up with a service no one wants. Your MVP must provide enough value that people are willing to buy it. After all, the only proof that they will pay for your solution is when they actually do.

MVPs are commonly used in the start-up world, and are especially popular in technology companies, but they're just as useful for law firms.

By testing your solution as an MVP, you'll:

- test demand and learn how your prospective clients react to your service

- save time and money – you'll only create the minimum product to start with, and future editions will be guided by client feedback so you can add features according to weight of demand

- gain valuable insight into what works and what doesn't as well as what people are willing to pay for.

TripAdvisor CMO Barbara Messing tests new product ideas by posting a banner advertisement on TripAdvisor's site.[7] If people click on the ad, they get a 404 (Not Found) error. If enough people click the ad, the product will go into development.

When we first launched our Probate On The Spot service, it was an MVP. The vision was to create custom-built software that would auto-mate the creation of the client's probate application. We'd collect the instructions and input them into the form during the conference, the software would generate the application and the client would sign it, all in the one consultation. As you might imagine, creating those fea-tures in our software was no small feat. We didn't want to spend time

---

7   hbr.org/2013/03/four-ways-to-market-like-a-sta.

and other resources on that until we knew that those efforts would be repaid.

For the first few months, we'd take the client's documents, give them a coffee and ask them to wait while we went into a different room and prepared their application manually. It wasn't long before we knew that not only did we have a great idea, it was one that people were willing to pay for. Only then did we spend the resources to develop the software functionality we needed.

Here's what this might look like for you:

- It might mean having an 'online service' that is completed manually behind the scenes, rather than being automated.

- It might be a brochure, landing page or email offering pre-orders for a product that you haven't built yet.

- It might be a topic and description for a training course, or a headline for a keynote presentation, before you've developed the product or written the speech.

As you receive feedback, you can refine your MVP and eventually build it out in full. When you get to this point, you'll have tested your service and know it will be a success.

In a buyer's market, the winners will be those who figure out what's working fastest, and do more of that, and figure out what's not working and get rid of it.

So, get to work on creating your MVP.

YOUR BESPOKE SERVICES

The most effective business model is one that offers a product ecosystem made up of a range of predefined and fixed-priced productised services alongside bespoke services.

Flagship products are about reducing your service to the 'lowest common denominator'; packaging a product that suits the needs of most of your clients or that is their entry-level service to your law firm. Of course, this service won't suit everyone's needs. That's where bespoke work comes in.

When we launched our Probate On The Spot service we were concerned that the simplicity of the product would turn off potential clients who had more complex affairs. What we saw, though, was the opposite. Our fixed price products position us as the experts in the practice area. There's no doubting that we know probate. This led to an increase in more complex work. Rather than trying to create a product for every possible scenario, instead we customise a quote for bespoke work. This gives us the opportunity to charge for that service based on the value we provide.

You should think of your bespoke work as a custom-designed legal product. You still need to determine a clear scope of works and set a price, but you won't have a predetermined system for delivery. This isn't about broadening your practice areas, but customising your service within your area of expertise.

You should charge for your bespoke work on a value pricing basis. Advertising your fixed (menu) prices for your flagship productised services helps to position the value you provide in your custom engagements.

SHOULD I ADVERTISE MY PRICES?

There are mixed views about whether lawyers should advertise their prices online. Even today, very few firms adopt this strategy. In my view, if you're going to adopt menu pricing, you should publish those prices on your website.

Picture this. It's Saturday evening. It's been a busy week and you've finally decided to organise some of that outsourcing you've been thinking about. You can't do everything. It's time to hire a cleaner.

You browse a few websites until you come across someone who looks trustworthy. You like their style. They're eco-friendly and have great reviews. The only problem? There's no price on their website. You want to tick this off your list. If you don't organise it now another month will pass and you'll be back at square one.

You umm and ahh for far too long and eventually settle on your second choice. Not quite as impressive as the first, but at least you know what it will cost – they have their prices on their website. You fill in their booking form and arrange a fortnightly clean starting Monday. Done.

Now, think back to your website.

Are you hiding your prices too?

If outsourcing isn't your thing, replace 'cleaner' with 'fancy new dress', 'golf clubs' or whatever you like to spend your hard-earned money on.

Are you giving your potential clients all the information they need to make a decision to buy from you?

If you charge a fixed price for your legal services you should advertise the price you charge. Below are some reasons why.

Create transparency

Lawyers and transparent pricing don't typically go hand in hand. When most people think 'lawyer' and 'price', they think 'hourly rate', 'expensive', 'overcharging' and 'unknown'.

Create transparency around your service offering by publishing your prices. Clients want to know what they're going to pay.

Differentiate your services

Most of the lawyers I work with charge on a fixed or value basis, so it's easy for me to fall into the trap of thinking everyone does things this way. But not everyone does. In fact, it's still more common for lawyers to charge on a timed basis than to quote a fixed price.

So even though you might not see fixed pricing as something that differentiates your service, it does.

Don't just tell people that you charge fixed fees, show them. Go that extra step and publish your prices on your website.

Attract the right clients

Ideally, you've priced your services at an amount that's right for your target market. You know who you want to serve and what those people are willing to pay. Are you the low-cost provider? Or are you the market-leading expert who clients pay a premium to access?

By advertising your prices you help your clients self-select. If you're way out of their price range, or even too low, they'll know to move on and find someone else.

Test your market's price point

If you haven't worked out the right price point for your target market, what better way to test it out than by telling people what you charge?

If you're concerned that publishing your prices will mean that they're set in stone, don't be. The price is just a number on a website. If you want to change it, log on and change it. Simple.

Save time on sales

Give prospective clients everything they need to make a buying decision on your website. They're busy. They want to make the decision when it suits them. Tell them everything they need to know. Not just your price, but what you'll do, how you'll deliver, when you'll do it and why they should choose you.

This way, when a prospective client does call you, they've been pre-sold by the information on your website. I find one of two things happens. Either they're ready to buy and want to get started (in which case they'll probably book online through your website if you give them the choice). Alternatively, they want to investigate you and make sure you're trustworthy. Often they'll ask you questions like, 'It says on your website that … is that right?' They want to make sure there's a human on the other side and once they've made sure of that, they're in.

Either way, you'll save time on answering questions about price.

* * *

The reluctance to advertise prices usually comes down to one of two things.

The first is the concern about losing prospective clients who will baulk at your price before you've had a chance to demonstrate your value. If you're worried about this then it's time to take another look at your website. Perhaps it isn't doing a good job of demonstrating your value. Can you add testimonials, share results you've helped your clients achieve, explain the features of your service, explain why you're unique, or value-add by providing helpful information.

The other concern is that people will take your price and shop around. Clearly showing the value of your offer is one way to prevent this. But also ask yourself whether the price-shoppers are really the people you're targeting anyway.

If you're clear about the market you serve and the value you provide, putting your prices on your website is a good thing.

ARE YOU READY TO ESCAPE THE BILLABLE HOUR?

Changing the way you package and charge for services isn't as simple as putting a price tag on a service; it's a whole business model change. When you change the way you charge, suddenly a whole host of other things start to change too, from the way you interact with clients to the way you measure and reward staff performance to the way you deliver services and manage knowledge.

Fixed pricing removes the dependence on time. When you've promised a client you'll complete the work within a set price, you've reframed the problem. Suddenly you're far more interested in working out how to streamline work, how to improve processes and complete work more efficiently.

Your flagship productised services work together with your bespoke services to create a product ecosystem of related and connected products that each solve problems for your clients. Your products support each other and coexist in a way that makes them stronger and more useful for clients as well as making them easier to sell. After delivering your flagship product you can continue to meet your client's needs by offering them other products in your ecosystem.

KEY POINTS IN THIS CHAPTER

1. A productised service has a predefined scope, fixed price and a system or method for delivery.

2. Products make it easier to sell and deliver legal services without depending on you. They also simplify the buying decision for clients and help to deliver a better client experience.

3. A product ecosystem is made up of a combination of flagship products and bespoke services, each providing a defined scope of services that solve your clients' problems.

 ## IT'S TIME TO DO LAW DIFFERENTLY

- Design your flagship products with a predefined scope, fixed price and system for delivery.

- Explore different pricing options to determine which is the best fit for your products and clients.

- If you choose menu pricing, don't hide your prices. Advertise them on your website.

- Create your MVP and start selling it. You can make improvements along the way.

Step 5:
Embrace modern marketing

'In every line of copy we write, we're either serving the customer's story or descending into confusion; we're either making music or making noise.'

Donald Miller, Author, *Building a StoryBrand*

FIND YOUR VISION   DEEPLY UNDERSTAND YOUR CLIENTS   CREATE AMAZING SOLUTIONS   PRODUCTISE YOUR SERVICES   EMBRACE MODERN MARKETING   OPTIMISE YOUR OPERATIONS

Law firm marketing used to consist of building referral networks and an ad in the *Yellow Pages*. The exclusivity of the legal profession meant lawyers didn't have to try too hard to find work. But as you well know, the game has changed. Control has shifted from law firms to buyers of legal services, and traditional marketing is no longer vital for success.

Traditionally, law firms have adopted *outbound* marketing, which involved sending broad messages to a wide, mostly uninterested audience. Think *Yellow Pages* and TV and radio ads. This type of marketing is one way, not highly targeted, and disrupts whatever the consumer is doing.

Modern marketing (also known as *inbound* marketing) is about attracting prospects who are actively looking for the solutions you provide. Instead of pushing a general message to a large audience, it's about making sure clients can find you when they need you. Modern marketing techniques focus on the online world. They include websites, social media, email marketing, content strategies, pay-per-click advertising and search engine optimisation. These strategies are designed to draw potential clients in by educating them and shedding light onto their problem and your solution through quality content, rather than outwardly pushing your brand in the *hope* that your message hits the right ears. More specifically, when a potential client asks Google about their problem, they find your website, full of valuable help, guidance and resources, and information about your productised services.

One of the best things about inbound marketing, especially email marketing, is that it's largely 'set and forget'. Once you've built a good lead magnet and email nurture sequence, your marketing leads will start to flow like a steady tap. You don't have to think about it every day and you can trust that your content is out there doing its job. Our most successful marketing campaign was built in 2017 and is still going strong. Other than a few tweaks to Google Ads, we haven't touched the basic content since it was created. (If you feel like I'm speaking another language, don't worry – I'll teach you about these things in this chapter.)

The success of modern marketing depends on a deep understanding of your ideal client (which we've already looked at) and providing valuable content to the client right at the moment they need it. I know you've got the first element down pat, so let's look at how you provide valuable content to the right people at the right time and how to translate that into clients and revenue for your law firm.

HOW TO CREATE YOUR MODERN MARKETING STRATEGY

The aim of your marketing strategy is to get potential clients to find you, know you, like you and trust you so that – ultimately – they will pay you.

There are four essential elements for creating your modern marketing strategy:

- Developing a strong elevator pitch.

- Building an engaging and useful website.

- Creating an appealing lead magnet and nurture campaign.

- Connecting with potential clients with the right material at the right time so that they visit your website.

We'll explore each of these below.

Develop your elevator pitch

You might have come across the idea of an elevator pitch or value proposition statement – a few succinct sentences that describe your business and can be delivered quickly, in the time it takes to travel in an elevator. A good elevator pitch helps spark interest in what your business does and clearly articulates your promise to your potential clients.

It explains:

- who you serve – your target market
- how you solve your clients' problems and improve their situation
- what benefits you provide
- what makes you different and why prospective clients should choose you over your competitors.

Sound familiar? You've done all the hard work on this in steps two and three, so there's no need to reinvent the wheel. All you need to do now is to pull that together into a few short, precise sentences.

Here are some examples:

- The Remote Expert: 'Take your online business from struggle street to supercharged. Only The Remote Expert combines online business strategy with legal expertise to help you grow your online business.'

- Hitch Advisory: 'Legal advice for business. Uncomplicated, relevant, expert advice. For too long legal and business advisors have been reactive and failed to demonstrate value to clients. Our mission is to empower your business and add value in every engagement. We are the experts in Retail, Business Law and Mergers and Acquisitions – and we're business people, too.'

- Sprintlaw: 'Re-imagining legal services for small business. Sprintlaw is a new type of law firm that operates completely online and on a fixed-fee basis. We're on a mission to make quality legal services faster, simpler and more affordable for small business owners and entrepreneurs.'

- 3D HR Legal: 'We help owners of professional services businesses prosper by creating thriving workplace cultures. Take your team from people problems to teams that get results by ensuring you are legally compliant and empowering your leaders to handle difficult conversations.'

The formulas below will help you craft your value proposition. Experiment with them and choose the one that works best for you:

- We help X do Y by Z.

- For [ideal client category] who [describe need] our [product/service name] is [product category] that [describe benefit].

- For [ideal client category] who [describe problem] we provide [describe solution] that [describe benefits] unlike [the competition] who [describe competition solution] our company [describe your better approach, solution and benefits] that [offers a better customer experience].

Your elevator pitch should be used on your website and in your marketing materials, so you'll need to spend some time crafting it to make sure you get it right. You'll also need to test it with your ideal clients to make sure it hits the mark.

Once you've got it right, use it everywhere: when you introduce yourself, as the headline on your website, on your business card and email footer, and in your marketing materials. Don't worry about overdoing it – you want the message to sink in.

Build an engaging and useful website

Law firm websites are notorious for being outdated and unappealing. Many are little more than big blocks of text explaining where staff went to law school and what areas of law they practice. This will no longer cut it.

Your website is your most important digital asset. It's the equivalent of your shop front in the real world. Having a well-designed, functional, modern website is non-negotiable. But a great website goes beyond having visual appeal and being mobile friendly, though these things are essential. The two most important roles your website plays are to explain what you do and to house your content.

Let's have a look at these.

What you do

Your website needs to expand on your elevator pitch, demonstrating your understanding of your clients' problems and how you can solve them.

Most lawyers' websites offer little more than a list of practice areas and staff capabilities and, as we've discovered in the Productise and Profit system, this is the wrong approach. Your website should be about your clients, not about you.

In *Building a StoryBrand: Clarify your message so customers will listen*, Donald Miller explains that businesses should adopt a story framework in their marketing efforts that positions their clients as the hero and their business as the guide, helping the hero to navigate the challenges ahead. Visitors to a website should be able to answer the following three questions within the first few minutes of arriving:

1. What do you offer?

2. How will it make my life better?

3. What do I need to do to buy it?

Housing your content

At the heart of modern marketing is content: blogs, videos, infographics, podcasts, guides and ebooks. You can demonstrate your expertise and position your business as the go-to by publishing quality content that speaks to your clients' problems and offers valuable information or advice.

The thought of content marketing is anxiety-inducing for many lawyers. After all, many law firm business models are built around an imbalance of power in relation to access to information – why give it away for free?!

As I explained earlier, we're in the Information Age where anyone can access information quickly, easily and at very little or even no cost. Information is out there anyway. If clients don't find it from you, they'll find it from someone else. Often potential clients want to see enough to know that you're the expert, that you know more than them, that they can trust you, and that you can help with their problem. When they're satisfied with this, they're happy to pay you to take over.

Miller agrees with this approach:

> *Create reciprocity. I've never worried about giving away too much free information. In fact, the more generous a brand is, the more reciprocity they create. All relationships are give-and-take, and the more you give to your customers, the more likely they will be to give something back in the future. Give freely.*

Your website is your home on the internet, and all your online marketing efforts should ultimately direct people to your website.

Is your website easy to read? Is it visually appealing? Does it explain who you are and what you do? Does it demonstrate your understanding of your client's problems? Does it position you as an authority? Do you use it to share valuable content?

Create an appealing lead magnet and nurture campaign

A good lead magnet is one of the most powerful tools you can use to market your business.

How many times have you given your email address in exchange for a free ebook, checklist or guide? You may not have realised that by doing so you were signing yourself up for lead nurturing by the business who gave you the freebie.

It works like this. You offer something of value to your customers – think ebook, guide, checklist, webinar or video course. In exchange for accessing your resource, your prospective client gives you their email address. You then sign them up to a nurture campaign – a series of emails that demonstrate your understanding of their problem and how you can help. This is all done through software that automates the whole process; once it's set up, the emails are sent automatically.

Examples of lead magnets include:

- text-based content such as how-to guides, reports, cheat sheets, checklists, case studies

- video content such as video guides and courses

- infographics

- widgets that provide customised reports or other information

- quizzes

- online demonstrations or free trials.

We use lead magnets in many of our marketing campaigns. Once upon a time, we'd charge clients for the kind of information contained in these documents. Now, though, we recognise that the content is far more valuable as a free resource that drives awareness of our services and builds trust and credibility with potential clients.

Your lead magnet should:

- Be valuable enough to encourage potential clients to give you their email address in exchange for it.

- Solve a problem for your ideal clients. It needs to be useful. Don't make a big promise only to deliver vague information that simply tries to upsell. That will produce the opposite effect. A good rule of thumb is to feel slightly uncomfortable at the thought you might have given away too much.

- Qualify your audience. Make it specific to your ideal client. There's no point building an email list of hundreds of people who are never going to become your clients.

- Be well designed. Don't send a poorly formatted, black-and-white Word document. Invest in graphic design and make sure your lead magnet looks great.

- Demonstrate your elevator pitch or value proposition. Your goal is to convince potential clients that they should buy from you, not your competitors.

Once you've captured your ideal client's email address, you can then 'nurture' them. This involves creating an automated email sequence that is specifically designed to educate, build awareness of your business and its products, and build trust in you as they progress along their customer journey.

Broadly speaking, that client journey looks like this:

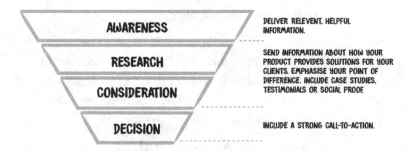

Your campaign should start by delivering relevant, valuable information and move towards clearer calls to action as they progress on this journey.

Delivering this kind of information directly to your prospective client's email inbox lets you build credibility by giving something of value and staying top of mind through helpful emails that remind them that you exist.

You don't need to reinvent the wheel – you can link to blog posts and other content that you've already created. Consider:

- blog posts that deal with your ideal client's problem
- content addressing your clients' objections to your solution
- case studies or social proof.

There are no rules about how many emails your campaign should include. Aim for 5 to 10 to get you started.

Connect with potential clients with the right material at the right time

This all sounds great, but how do you get people to your website and lead magnet in the first place? There are three main strategies you can use to help potential clients find you: social media, search engine optimisation and pay-per-click advertising.

Social media

Social media should be used to amplify your message and lead potential clients to your website. It offers the opportunity to distribute your content to a wider audience and to humanise your brand.

Start by working out where your ideal clients spend their time online and build your presence there. There's no point having a beautiful Instagram feed if your clients are mostly on LinkedIn.

Your aim should be for potential clients to find you, know you, like you and trust you. This requires you to share information that's of interest and value to your clients in a way that they want to consume it. Just as your products don't need to be limited to legal advice, neither does your content. Here's an opportunity to demonstrate the depth of your understanding about your ideal client.

Rizwana McDonald, Director of Foundd Legal, gets most of her new business from her Instagram and Facebook platforms. She works for creatives and startups who use these platforms for their own businesses. Foundd Legal shows up online consistently, and focuses on freely sharing practical and strategic business information that their ideal clients need to know.[1]

Clarissa Rayward is another example of a lawyer leading the way with social media. Her firm, Brisbane Family Law Centre, gets a significant

---

1 Rizwana and I discuss this on episode 62 of the Doing Law Differently podcast.

portion of new business from the awareness of her brand that comes from her presence on social media.

As well as organic posting, you can also use social media for paid advertising and target your advertisements to reach your ideal audience. Your ads can link directly to your lead magnet download page to get visitors to sign up to your nurture campaign.

Search engine optimisation

Google's Zero Moment of Truth research confirms that people make buying decisions in what Google call the Zero Moment, the precise moment when they have a need, intent or question they want answered online. To optimise your marketing, you need to show up at these moments and have something interesting, relevant or engaging to say.

Search engine optimisation (SEO) is about making your website show up higher in search engine results. The better your SEO, the higher your website will rank when potential clients search key terms that relate to your services. SEO is affected by the speed of your website, whether it is mobile friendly, and how well your pages are optimised for your keywords among other things. The more content you produce that relates to the problems your ideal clients are searching, the more likely they'll find you in an organic search listing at their Zero Moment.

Pay-per-click advertising

Pay-per-click advertising (PPC) campaigns give you control over what keywords your website ranks for and what page of your website prospects are led to. If your SEO isn't up to scratch yet, PPC can help you rank higher in search engine results.

Google Ads enable you to get in front of your ideal clients when they're searching on Google. If the goal of modern marketing is to make sure potential clients can find you when they need you, Google Ads does a brilliant job of achieving that goal.

Google Ads can be a valuable source of new business, but they don't operate in isolation and depend heavily on the ad linking to a useful and attractive website, appealing lead magnet and nurture campaign and, of course, a great product offering too.

MARKETING DOESN'T STOP WHEN YOU GET A PAYING CLIENT

From the way you show up online and in the real world to the way you engage with your clients throughout your service delivery and how you interact with them afterwards, *everything* you do in your business is a form of marketing.

You want your clients to become promoters of your company, and to do that you need to deliver on the promises you've made throughout their journey so far.

When your hear the words 'customer experience', you might be more likely to think of the last time you got passed around a call centre or copped some attitude from a retail shop employee than you are to think about what it's like for your clients to engage with your service, but customer experience is just as relevant to law firms as it is to call centres, flight check-in and software.

Traditionally, lawyers have focused on the practice of law: understanding legislation, legal theory and legal process, applying the law to factual circumstances and representing parties in litigation. In this book, I argue you need to be focused on the business of law, and as part of that you need to understand the *experience* of law.

Client experience is a client's perception of the experience they have with your business. It's formed by every interaction they have with you, from when they find you on Google to when they receive your final bill.

Someone who has a positive experience is more likely to be a repeat and loyal client. Not only that, they're more likely to recommend your business to others, too. *How* you deliver is just as important as *what* you deliver.

Why does it matter? Well, in our buyer's market, if we don't make it easy and pleasant to do business with us, clients will simply choose to go elsewhere.

The good news, though, is that the better experience you provide, the more likely your clients are to recommend you to others. The Net Promoter Score (NPS) metric measures how likely clients are to refer your service to others by asking them a simple question: 'How likely is it that you would recommend [Organization X/Product Y/Service Z] to a friend or colleague?'

Customers answer with a rating between 0 (not at all likely) and 10 (extremely likely). Depending on their response, customers fall into one of three categories to establish an NPS:

- Promoters (9 or 10) – typically loyal and enthusiastic customers.

- Passives (7 or 8) – they are satisfied with your service but not happy enough to be considered promoters.

- Detractors (0 to 6) – unhappy customers who are unlikely to buy from you again, and may even discourage others from buying from you.

Your goal is to convert your customers into promoters and keep your promoters happy.

In days gone by, if a person needed legal advice, they'd need to write a letter, make a phone call or visit the office in person. These traditional ways of providing legal services don't always suit the modern buyer, and they often act as barriers to engaging your services in the first place. Clients expect to be served on demand and instantly. Of course, not every area of law lends itself to the ability to be delivered in this way, but aspects of the service may – and those aspects may be enough to make a client choose your firm over another.

In our modern, increasingly connected world, clients aren't just comparing your service with other lawyers, they're comparing you to other service providers too. They compare having to telephone your office during business hours to arrange an appointment to making a booking with their GP after-hours via a web form from the comfort of their sofa. They compare compiling information and filling in your lengthy capture forms by hand with their annual tax return completed via an online form.

As the authors of *Service Design: From insight to inspiration* put it, 'the design of services is becoming a key competitive advantage. Physical elements and technology can easily be copied, but service experiences are rooted in company culture and are much harder to replicate.'

We all experience first-hand examples of good and bad service daily. We've come to expect top service everywhere we go and across all industries. Customer expectations are increasing. Being competent and delivering on time are the bare basics. To provide excellent service you need to do much more than deliver the basics. You need to enable customers to do business where, when and how they want in ways that are simple, consistent and relevant.

Author and legal services industry advisor Mitchell Kowalski agrees, saying that the 'real competitive advantage for lawyers [comes] from delivering legal services in a way that [is] different from their competitors.'[2]

Try these three things:

1. **Provide a fast, hassle-free experience and differentiate on ease.** Our Wills On The Spot service has continued to grow organically as a result of the hassle-free experience. Clients can make an appointment with our lawyers online, show up to their appointment, and leave 45 minutes later with a will professionally prepared, signed, witnessed and stored in safe custody. It's hassle free, fast and convenient.

2. **Exceed expectations. Delight your customers by going the extra mile.** A common misconception is that 'going the extra mile' comes at a big expense, but this doesn't have to be the case.

   Resolve Estate Law is a boutique law firm based in Brisbane, founded by Zinta Harris. The firm practises in contested deceased estate matters. The first words you see on their website are 'Compassion, when you need it most'. They clearly understand that their clients are looking for help with much more than the law. Their clients are people whose loved one has recently died, and who now find themselves disagreeing with family over the estate. Not only are they grappling with a legal process, they're also dealing with challenging emotions that come from a family dispute. They're trying to resolve legal, family, financial, moral and emotional issues all at once.

   At your first meeting with Resolve, you'll be given a copy of Zinta's book, *Rest In Peace: How to manage an estate dispute without inheriting heartache*, an essential oil roller and some beautifully packaged tea leaves. This is part of Resolve's 'calm and caring

---

2   Mitchell Kowalski – The Great Legal Reformation p133.

guidance' approach to estate law. Zinta says: *'It is all part of my approach to have clients understand that they need support in every facet when they face their curveball moment. In giving them the oil and the tea I encourage them to take time out to think about what is most important to them, to picture what their "forever altered new normal" might look like – and to practise daily calmness. It empowers my clients to best survive what is a harrowing time.'*[3]

How reassuring to know that your lawyer is looking after your interests as a whole person, not just your legal matter.

3. **Take note of service experiences that you find frustrating and do the opposite in your business.** We've all experienced the transfer between departments in a call centre, having to identify ourselves and explain our problem over and over. How refreshing is it when the person you're transferred to knows your problem and just gets on with helping you? How can you emulate this in your business?

    I heard a great example of what *not* to do when a friend shared that her lawyer had her (the client's) name as the subject line of every email and attached the content in a PDF document, rather than putting it in the body of the email. This was not only frustrating and impersonal, but also made it impossible for her to search through previous emails. What could your business learn from this?

---

3   Learn more about Resolve Estate Law in episode 8 of the Doing Law Differently podcast.

KEY POINTS IN THIS CHAPTER

1. Instead of pushing a general message to a large audience, the goal of modern marketing is to make sure clients can find you when they need you.

2. Get potential clients to find you, know you, like you and trust you by publishing quality content that educates, informs and helps your client to solve their problem.

3. Use social media to amplify your message, but direct potential clients to your website where you can deliver a lead magnet, capture their email address and add them to a nurture campaign.

4. Marketing doesn't stop when a new client signs up. Their whole experience with you is an opportunity to promote your business.

 ## IT'S TIME TO DO LAW DIFFERENTLY

- Develop your elevator pitch, memorise it, and include it on your website, marketing materials and social media platforms.

- Make sure your website is up to scratch.

- Create a lead magnet and email nurture campaign.

- Decide how you'll attract potential clients to your website and develop your marketing campaign.

Step 6:
Optimise your operations

'And that, I believe, is the heart of process: not efficiency,
not effectiveness, not more money, not to "downsize"
or "get lean", but to simply and finally create more life
for everyone who comes into contact with the business,
but most of all, for you, the person who owns it.'

Michael E. Gerber, *The E-Myth*

FIND YOUR VISION · DEEPLY UNDERSTAND YOUR CLIENTS · CREATE AMAZING SOLUTIONS · PRODUCTISE YOUR SERVICES · EMBRACE MODERN MARKETING · OPTIMISE YOUR OPERATIONS

The last step in the Productise and Profit process is to optimise your operations. This step is all about looking at the behind-the-scenes of your business to improve the way it runs. Your goal is to reduce dependency on you, to get your business operating like a well-oiled machine.

THE FOUR ESSENTIAL ELEMENTS TO OPTIMISING YOUR BUSINESS OPERATIONS

For many years, *people*, *process* and *technology* have been recognised as the three components of successful operational change. In today's Information Age, I think we need to add 'knowledge' as the fourth component.

As a professional worker, most of your value is in your head. The only way to reduce your business's dependence on you is to extract, document, organise and optimise that information. Essential to your operations, then, is the ability to manage that knowledge for the use and benefit of other people. If you want to reshape your firm and regain your life, it's hard to argue that knowledge should not become the fourth component of successful strategy.

The 'people, process, technology golden triangle' can become the 'people, process, knowledge, technology diamond'. Together, these four elements are essential to optimising your business operations to create an efficient and effective business model that leaves you time for the other priorities in life. No single element operates in isolation:

- Having the right **people** with the right skills is the starting point. People do the work. Without people to drive a business, nothing happens.

- **Processes** help people do better work. Processes are a series of steps that need to happen to achieve a particular outcome.

Processes are put in place to optimise people's work and prevent them from reinventing the wheel every time they work.

- **Knowledge** is all the information that is stored in the brains of the people and implicit in the systems. If that knowledge only exists in your head, how can you ever expect to take a holiday and let your business run well while you're away?

- **Technology** helps people work faster, better and cheaper. It lets us automate the grunt work and free up people's time for more creative or strategic work, or even just to work *less* and do something else with that time.

Balance is essential. If you don't have proper processes in place, your people won't work optimally. Technology needs to fit your business processes, and your people need to be able to operate it. And if you want other people to operate your business for you, they need to be able to make use of all that knowledge that's in your head.

Optimising these four elements is the last step on your journey to Productise and Profit. Let's take a closer look at each of these.

IF YOU BUILD THE PEOPLE, THEY WILL BUILD THE BUSINESS

Managing, leading, training and employing people can be one of the most rewarding parts of your business, but it can also be the cause of some of your biggest headaches.

I asked one law firm owner to tell me her biggest challenge and biggest reward about running her firm. Her answer to both was the same: 'my team'. It's a double-edged sword. Having a united front to take your business out into the world to tackle your big 'why' is far more powerful and enjoyable than doing it alone. At the same time, how many hours a week do you spend dealing with HR issues that you wish would just go away?

But if you truly want to reshape your business and regain your life, you can't do it alone. Tapping into the potential of your people, sharing the load and drawing on skills you don't have is an essential part of the journey. Even if your vision doesn't include employing large teams of lawyers, you still need people on your team to move your business forward. The different skills and strengths, perspectives and interests that other individuals bring to the table are crucial to enable you to spend your time doing what is most valuable to you.

I often say that the success I've had in my career is down to my ability to delegate. I'm good at teaching others to do my job, making myself redundant and then moving on to the next thing. This is the approach you need to take too and the best way to do it is to build a thriving team and culture that acts as the bedrock of your business.

Why culture matters – a lot

You've heard it said that people are a business's most important asset. This is especially true in law. The knowledge you profit from exists mostly in people's brains (although hopefully by the time you finish this chapter you'll be working on getting your IP out of people's brains and into a more tangible form!).

Your people are on the frontline, engaging with clients and representing your brand. They bring skills and knowledge that are essential to delivering your services and, in some cases, years of experience in the way things are done.

There's no denying that people make a big impact on business performance, but while we know this, we're often so busy keeping up with the day-to-day demands of business that we don't prioritise people in the way we should.

Let's be honest – law doesn't have a good reputation when it comes to culture. Long work hours, high billable targets, hierarchies and competition are seen as just part of the job, but they're a part that contributes to poor workplace culture. Even if you've done away with billable targets and long work hours in your practice, law is a serious job. Our day-to-day actions have significant implications for people's lives, and that in itself can cause high levels of stress.

The high costs of staff turnover

Having a good culture also means staff are less likely to leave your employment. Staff turnover isn't always a bad thing, but there's a big difference between losing a disgruntled, underperforming employee and losing a highly valued, high-performing employee. It's easy to disregard the costs associated with a single employee who leaves your employment, but if you were to do some quick maths, you might be shocked at the result. The costs of staff turnover can be substantial.

While the direct costs like recruiter fees and insurance are obvious, there are many indirect costs and business disruptions that aren't so easily quantified, and which often go unnoticed or unaccounted for. For a start, think about all the time you spend dealing with staff issues: performance management, file handover and training new staff. Add to this the setbacks from lost productivity, flow-on effects on staff morale and all the IP that walks out the door when your staff member leaves.

According to the Macquarie Bank *2020 Legal Services Industry Pulse Check*, 82% of firms say attracting and keeping staff will be a key challenge over the next two years. It's no surprise, given that the average annual turnover rate in the legal profession is 21% for fee earners and 26% for support staff.[1] This means that in just 4.76 years the entire staff of a firm may have been replaced.

---

1   alpma.com.au/resources/2019-alpma-australian-legal-industry-salary-hr-issues-survey.

Having a strong, positive workplace culture impacts happiness and job satisfaction. It will drive your team's engagement and performance, and is hugely important to the success and overall health of your business. People are happier and more engaged when they're valued as people, not as billable units. This means that you need to find ways to make work more meaningful, purposeful and engaging for people.

Finding the right people

If you have the right people in the right places in your business then you can create systems that remove you as the bottleneck and let you spend your time on other priorities.

So, what skills are you looking for?

There are many different competency models that try to pinpoint the skills a modern lawyer needs to have:

- The T-shaped lawyer – a lawyer who has deep legal expertise but also has a solid grounding in another subject, be it technology, business, analytics, human resources, design or many others.

- The Delta Model[2] recognises that lawyers need knowledge, skills and abilities related to:

  - people: understanding and relating to clients, colleagues and self

  - process: delivering legal services efficiently and effectively

  - practice: knowing, researching and clearly communicating the law.

---

2   alysoncarrel.com/delta-competency-model.

- The O-shaped lawyer[3] adopts a 'people first, then lawyers' approach and recognises five mindsets that a modern lawyer should have:
  - optimism: having a positive mindset
  - ownership: taking accountability for outcomes
  - open-minded: having an open, growth mindset
  - opportunistic: taking opportunity where appropriate, rather than avoiding risks
  - original: creative and innovative problem solving.

While these are useful, the most practical thing you can do is to work out where your own strengths and weaknesses lie and what tasks would be better done by someone else.

Across your business, you need people whose skills match the four business elements: the business of law, the practice of law, legal operations and people.

The people on your team won't necessarily be lawyers. The practice of law is just one element. Many of the roles in our firm are filled by competent and enthusiastic law students and other professionals. Our team has also comprised web developers, software developers, accountants, designers, marketers and other professionals.

In *Law is a Buyer's Market*, Jordan Furlong contemplates a future where lawyers are no longer essential to law firms:

> *The model is now, slowly, giving way to a new vision of law firms,*
> *one that revolves not around lawyers, but around the firm's*
> *capacity to deliver services of value to clients. This new law*
> *firm's 'engine room' is not comprised of collected lawyers, but of*

---

3   oshapedlawyer.com/about/#framework.

collected legal expertise, *applied to client needs through the use of systems, processes, technology and expert professionals as well as lawyers.*

I'm not suggesting that you rid your firm of lawyers, rather that lawyers aren't the only means to the end. Furlong adds:

The goal of successful law firms in the new market is not to dispense with lawyers, but to use lawyers appropriately and proportionately in order to maximize the overall productivity of the firm and the value it provides to clients.

Keeping the right people

Here are some of the lessons I've learnt over 10 years leading teams in law, which will help you keep the right people on your team:

- Work with your team to design their roles around their strengths and aspirations. Don't squeeze a person into a position just because you need to fill it. Instead, encourage them to bring their strengths and passions to their work in a way that fulfills them. Finding the crossover between staff interests and business needs means everybody wins.

- Set simple, team-based KPIs. Over the last few years we've helped our teams to set their own team-based KPIs. We bring each team together every six months to talk about what's going well, areas for improvement, and what they want to focus on for the next six months. They set the goals as a team and choose a team-based reward if they achieve them. People have much more buy-in and are more interested in seeing plans succeed when they're part of creating them.

- Don't overcomplicate individual performance reviews. We changed our performance reviews from a complete overview of every possible aspect of performance, carried out by completing a multi-page review document followed by a meeting, to a simple conversation looking at five issues:

  – A review of the KPIs and goals set at the previous meeting.

  – What's going well?

  – What are your areas for improvement?

  – What are your career goals?

  – What are your goals for the next 12 months?

- Billable work isn't the only measure of success. As you move away from tracking hours as you develop your product-based business, the way you measure performance changes too. Contribution to business development, innovation, process improvement, marketing, product development, management and many others are just as important.

- Help your staff to live their best life in and out of work by supporting and encouraging flexible work.

- Encourage staff to engage with professional bodies and volunteer committees. Help them to understand life outside your firm so they don't need to leave your employment to discover if the grass is greener on the other side.

- Pay your people well, but also recognise that money isn't everything. Get to know what your team values most. For example, our team, like most, I suspect, enjoy fancy lunches.

- Hire quickly and fire fast. A bad egg can have a detrimental and outsized effect on your team.

It's time to do leadership differently

Good management and leadership is one of the most effective methods for employee engagement. Employers and managers have the power to mentor, develop and inspire people to achieve great things.

Leadership in law has traditionally been about trying to extract the most out of people. But good leadership is about inspiring the best in people. This style of leadership, known as conscious leadership, is about changing the focus from 'me' to 'we'. A conscious leader asks not just what an employee can give to them, but what they can give to the employee.

They know that their employees have so much more to their lives than just their work, and they want to support them with those other things too. They inspire and bring out the best in people, rather than intimidating them to work harder and draining them for all they can. They aim to use teamwork to meet everyone's objectives, putting people ahead of profits and prioritising a purpose bigger than their own organisation.

What's important from a business perspective though, is that conscious leadership is not only a good way to lead, it's a good way to do business as well.

According to author Dan Pink, the three things that matter most to employees are:

- autonomy – feeling a sense of ownership of their work

- mastery – the need for expertise in a field

- purpose – to feel as if they're contributing to something bigger than themselves.

Employees want more from their work than just a pay cheque. They want to feel that they matter and that the work they do matters.

REGAIN YOUR LIFE WITH PROCESSES AND SYSTEMS

Would you bake a cake without a recipe?

Maybe the answer is 'yes' if you're making a Victoria Sponge, but what about a Baked Alaska? A Soufleé? Crème Brûlée?

There's plenty that could go wrong. You might accidentally melt the ice cream, spill a little yolk in the egg whites or over-beat the eggs. Perhaps you'll overcook the edges or undercook the middle; or open the oven door just a little too early and watch your masterpiece sink.

There's a simple reason we follow a recipe when we bake: we want to achieve the best outcome in the most effective way. When you follow a recipe, you get the benefit of the lessons learnt by those who have come before you. Those who realised the importance of adding the ingredients in just the right order; using the whites, not the yolk; not leaving the mixture on the bench for too long; and making sure the oven door stays shut.

Now consider your legal work.

How often do you follow a recipe for your work? Before you get started on a new matter, do you look at your ingredients list and read through the method so you know what's ahead? Or do you just dive in, whisk at the ready, hoping for the best?

Systems are the business equivalent of a baking recipe. Effective business systems are the difference between a business that rises and one that sinks.

More than that, if you want someone else to take care of your business while you're not there, to rid yourself of the pressure of the day-to-day running of things, you'd better give them a recipe.

Seven ways systems can transform your business

When I started my journey creating and improving processes, I didn't fully appreciate just how significant it would be. What was initially born out of frustration has gone on to bring myriad benefits.

Let's take a look at some of the things you can do with good processes ...

1. Eliminate grunt work and increase productivity

Let's be honest, there are a lot of things you'd rather do than fixing formatting on a contract, copy and pasting advice on how to sign a document, or answering the same question for the third time today.

Here are some of the things I never have to do again, thanks to some good systems:

- **Attach documents to emails.** My document templates know what I want to attach and do it for me. Never again will I forget to attach a compulsory costs disclosure or have to go hunting for a list of authorised witnesses.

- **Check for faxes.** Yes, they're ancient, which means we sometimes forget they exist. Well, we truly can forget them now: we have a system that automatically checks the folder and imports the files into our practice management software.

- **Check the obituaries.** This is a real job that lawyers who store original wills are required to do, and one that we did manually for many years until we found a way to automatically check the obituary data against the data in our wills bank.

Good processes cut down on tedious, repetitive tasks that eat up critical working hours and brainpower. When you can automate a great process, staff are free to focus on more meaningful and enjoyable work, which leads to a happier workforce.

2. Improve the customer experience

When processes are intentionally designed with a focus on customer success from the beginning, they serve to enhance the customer experience. Great processes mean staff collect the right information at the right time, provide the right level of detail for any given task, can move efficiently between stages, and can take the client on a positive journey as they deliver the service.

Not only do good processes lead to a better customer experience, they can also highlight opportunities to cross-sell and up-sell services. This has the result of increasing revenue at a very low cost.

Done poorly, though, they can make your service worse. You want your clients to feel like they're being taken on a journey, not being processed through a factory.

3. Improve risk management

In our profession, the words 'risk management' are never far from the tip of the tongue.

Working ad hoc and not following a process increases the risk of human error. Even a manual process that has been thought through and documented will help to manage risk by acting as a simple checklist. If something falls outside the parameters of a process, that's enough to prompt you to question why and be alert for risk.

It was almost a rite of passage for every member of our conveyancing team to miss a duties lodgement deadline, a mistake which came hand in hand with hefty penalties.

I knew this costly human error could be eliminated with a decent process, so I automated a task that managed the lodgement date. One week before the due date, the system checks if the contract has been lodged, and if it hasn't, it sends a reminder to the file manager. It also produces a report of all the files in the system, showing their lodgement due date and status.

4. Enable work to be completed by staff with less experience

Process-driven work can be completed by less experienced staff much more effectively. Law firms can engage the lowest cost fit-for-purpose person to do a job. This means that clients don't pay a premium for a lawyer to do work that could be done by an administration clerk.

5. Improve quality through consistency and repeatability

I get a great deal of satisfaction out of making small improvements to a process or document template. Two minutes spent reordering tasks in a workflow, deleting unnecessary ones or fixing formatting errors on a template means no one will ever again have to fix those problems manually. Each time you use a process you can make minor tweaks to improve it.

This week we spent half a day improving our family law conveyancing process and templates, an investment in time that will save hundreds of hours, lead to a better client experience and improve the quality of our work.

6. Enhance staff training

Systems and processes make it much easier to train new staff. Rather than starting with a blank slate and attempting to explain every possible variation, you simply teach the process.

Better processes help staff understand more complex concepts more quickly because they are freed from the grunt work and are able to spend time thinking about and understanding the other issues.

Process-driven work is easier to supervise. Managers can see at a glance where a certain matter is up to, what steps have been completed and what has occurred that might fall outside the standard process.

7. Increase profits

The bottom line is that process improvement saves time and money, and now that you're selling value, not time, this is an excellent position to be in. The better you become at delivering work, the more profit you make and the more time you have. And the better the experience you provide for your clients, the more likely they are to return to you and to recommend you to others.

Six essential systems you need in your business

There are lots of different systems you can have in your business. Once you start implementing them and seeing these benefits for yourself, you'll want to systemise everything.

Here are six essential systems that will help you to reshape your business.

1. Marketing and lead generation

Regardless of where your work comes from, you need a system for generating more of it. Whether it's content creation for content marketing or meeting new people to build a referral network, having a system in place means you're more likely to succeed.

2. New enquiries and quotes

What's your system for dealing with new client enquiries?

If potential clients aren't treated with the level of service they expect *before* they engage you, what are the chances of them signing up to your services?

Consider: who on your team receives the new business enquiries? What is your system for making sure they're dealt with promptly? Do you have a booking system for new client appointments? What about a system to ensure that quotes are sent out promptly? Are your quotes followed up? When, and by whom?

3. Service delivery

Having read this far, you'll know that your productised services should be driven by a system for service delivery. Develop workflows and processes that guide staff through the process of delivering a service. Those systems will help you to deliver a seamless service experience for your customers.

4. Billing

Having a system around billing will help you to better manage your cashflow. What is your payment policy? Who is responsible for sending out bills, and at what frequency? Whose job is it to follow up payment? How do you handle overdue bills? Or, better yet, do you require money in trust in advance of services being provided?

5. Staff recruitment

Whether you handle recruitment internally or engage an agent, you'll still need a system to help you through the process – from writing and publishing a job ad to reviewing applications, interviewing, making an offer and induction. All these steps can be streamlined down to a simple system, ridding you of hassle when finding and hiring new staff.

6. Knowledge management

Although we're a profession steeped in precedent, we're far more likely to move on to the next piece of billable work than we are to take the time to record and store our knowledge so we can use it again. But unfortunately, our brains are not as reliable as we think, and that case you think you'll never forget will soon be buried deep underneath hundreds more.

What's your system for storing those clever strategies you develop, research you undertake or secret loopholes you discover?

Pay attention to the little things

Process improvement is something that I do every single day. A two-minute fix on 'document template formatting', for example, will save hours over each year by virtue of our staff not having to do it manually every time. It might sound excessive (or perhaps obsessive!), but this is exactly the mindset you need to encourage in your teams. You need to encourage a culture of constant, logical and sustainable improvement throughout your business. Continuous improvement needs to become a way of life, ingrained in the culture.

DON'T LET YOUR KNOWLEDGE LANGUISH OR WALK OUT THE DOOR

When faced with a document drafting challenge, I'm willing to bet that one of the first things you do is to look for a precedent. Why start with a blank slate when someone else has done this before? Lawyers hoard precedents like people hoarded toilet paper during COVID-19. Precedents are the method to the recipe for the practice of law. When tasked with the job of preparing a document, we go to our precedent library, choose the most appropriate document and get cracking, editing, reviewing and analysing, all with the benefit of the work done by someone else who walked this path before.

I'm sure we can all relate to the comfort that comes from pulling out a precedent. We don't have to reinvent the wheel, there's less chance that we'll forget an important clause or issue, and even if we adopt nothing more than the formatting, a precedent will save us a lot of grunt work.

Knowledge management

When it comes to document preparation, precedents are king, but when it comes to knowledge management more generally, we often drop the ball. We're knowledge workers, which means we work with information, much of which is in our heads. What we don't do so well is record that information in ways that let us use it time and time again.

What is knowledge management?

How often have you been faced with a legal issue that you knew you'd dealt with before, but you just couldn't put your finger on the name of the client or matter? You knew you'd come up with an excellent strategy, but now the research was buried deep in an old file, and you had no idea which one.

The most valuable asset of your law firm is the experience, knowledge and expertise of the people within it. Knowledge management is about leveraging your collective experience by storing, growing and sharing knowledge. It's about capturing your wisdom, past work, experiences, processes and policies and putting it all at the fingertips of your team, so it can be accessed and reused.

Knowledge management is about so much more than document precedents. It should include information about methods, techniques and approaches as well as documents, systems and processes. Think of precedents as the end result and the rest of your knowledge management as the way to achieve it.

The humble checklist

On 30 October 1935, two rival aeroplane companies gathered in an airfield in Ohio to pitch their planes against each other. The best performer would win a lucrative contract with the US Army Air Corps. The Boeing taxied onto the runway and rose into the sky, only to stall and nosedive into the ground, killing two of the crew. An investigation found that the crash was caused by the pilots taking off with locked controls. The plane was said to be too complicated, with the number of tasks required to take off and fly safely too much for human memory. Needless to say, Boeing didn't win the contract, but it did go on to work out how to avoid a similar tragedy occurring again.

Their solution was stunningly simple: a checklist. Everything the pilot needed to remember was written on an index card. After the checklist was introduced, Boeing was able to eventually sell their plane to the US Army Air Corps, where it flew for years without incident.

Today, checklists are mandatory tools used not just in aviation, but by surgeons, nurses, marketers, psychologists and many other industries.

Checklists are one of my favourite knowledge management tools for lawyers. If you're new to knowledge management, I suggest you start by creating a few simple checklists. Start by creating a basic onboarding checklist that sets out all the information you need from each new client or a checklist for the key milestones in your new productised services.

How do I do it?

You don't need a fancy software system to get started with knowledge management. We started with some basic file note summaries that we bound together. Today, I prefer an online system that can be updated quickly, is easily accessible and can be searched.

If you're just getting started, follow these steps.

1. Identify your critical systems and knowledge

Make a list of legal issues you have to think through often, topics that you find yourself consistently teaching to new staff or your most frequently asked questions.

2. Start simply

Start with a simple checklist of things you need to consider when dealing with that issue. Checklists are quick and easy to produce and can be updated and enhanced over time. As you start to develop your knowledge bank, add hyperlinks and references in your checklist to link it to other documents.

Other ideas include writing an article or blog for your firm's intranet, tagging your electronic files with a meaningful tag that you can search in the future, or keeping a simple file note with a brief description of issues along with links to documents, advices and files.

Knowledge sharing isn't just about written articles. Sometimes the most effective way to share information is by recording a short presentation, video or audio file. If I want to demonstrate a process, I often record my screen and voiceover. This is a much more effective way of showing someone else around a website or software process.

3. Be consistent

Whatever you choose, it's important to be consistent. It's no good keeping the file note if you never update it or creating a tag system but only half-heartedly adding tags. For knowledge management to work well, you need your team to embrace it. Create a template for your checklists and information sheets so they have a consistent visual design. Well-designed documents enable information to be absorbed more easily and are more likely to be used in the first place.

Make knowledge sharing a way of life in your business

As with many of the changes we've examined, knowledge management isn't a one time, set and forget. Knowledge management and knowledge sharing need to become a part of the way you work.

So how do you make knowledge sharing a way of life?

In day-to-day practice, we encourage staff to use and update our knowledge management systems. The more they feel ownership of them, the more likely they are to maintain them. If a team member asks me a question that is dealt with in a system, I send them there instead of giving them the answer. If they bring me a question that I don't know the answer to, they're tasked with researching it and writing a short info piece. It will probably then form the basis for staff training.

Contribution to knowledge management is recognised and rewarded in staff performance reviews. Establishing KPIs around it helps to make it a priority.

Don't let your IP walk out the door when your staff leave. Instead, make it part of their job to develop, update and improve your knowledge management. They may leave your employment, but at the very least you'll still get the benefit of the knowledge they acquired while working for you.

Effective knowledge management lets you capture and reuse your and your team's expertise in effective and transformative ways. It is much bigger than saving and searching for information, it's about saving time by applying the right knowledge to deliver services more effectively.

MAKING USE OF THE POWER OF TECHNOLOGY

You might be surprised to see that technology is the last item in my blueprint for the Productise and Profit system. There's no doubt that technology has and will continue to revolutionise the legal profession, but as you've seen from this book, it is just one of the factors at play.

I have a unique perspective on legal technology, having been a driving force in the development of our firm's legal practice management software, ContactsLaw. Unhappy with what the market had to offer, our firm set about creating its own practice management software. What followed was the creation of a revolutionary program built by software developers but designed, from day one, by lawyers.

I could fill the whole book with examples of features our firm has designed in direct response to challenges we face in practice, but what's far more interesting for you is how all this translates in your practice. Not everyone is lucky enough to have a software developer on their team, and you and I both know how quickly new technology comes and goes. So rather than tell you about specific tech tools, the aim here is to share what I've learned about legal technology and break it down to practical, actionable takeaways for you.

Will robots replace us?

The unnerving fear that robots will replace us often acts as a big roadblock that interferes with lawyers adopting new technology. We worry that if we automate our work then we'll be out of a job. Time billing provides little incentive to adapt, after all – we can charge more if it takes longer! Or so we think.

Technology might replace us in part. At the very least, it is replacing human work that is dull, dangerous, dirty and dear. Technology can replace the grunt work, and we are better for it. I can spend my time doing work I love, not paper-pushing and administrative tasks. But technology won't negate the need for educated and specialised professionals, for humans who can empathise with others.

In its 2018 report *Artificial Intelligence in Legal Practice*, the Centre for Legal Innovation at The College of Law concluded that:

> *AI has and will change the way lawyers work, the work they do, how it is done, where and why – these are largely positive changes for the profession. AI and technology more generally has and will continue to remove work from lawyers that they were arguably always overqualified and overpaid to do. What will be left is that lawyers will use AI and tech tools to assist them in applying their experience, judgment and arriving at creative solutions to complex problems that work within the context of a client's matter and is cognisant of all the implications that may ensue. Lawyers will be able to spend more time with clients and place even greater emphasis on personal interactions.*

Employment lawyer Jo Alilovic made this point perfectly at a presentation she gave at a law conference. Jo was addressing an audience of forward-thinking lawyers about how they could use people to scale their business. In her opening address, she said:

> *Do you know what's wonderful about tech? It doesn't need a sick day. It doesn't need time off for a sports carnival. It definitely doesn't need 12 months off to have a baby and it doesn't need a cry in the bathroom every now and then. But do you know what tech can't do: it can't do human, and every law firm needs human. Tech can't empathise. It can't see how a client is feeling. It can't give a hug when one is needed and it can't give suggestions and solutions based on all of those factors, not just the best technical, legal solution.*

Human relationships are still at the core of what we do. Technology can't replace humans.

Don't fall for the bells and whistles

I've experienced legal technology from all sides: lawyer and file owner, supervisor, practice manager, software developer, business advisor and customer. With such a rounded view, I've got a good feeling for what works and what doesn't. Time and time again, where I see people go wrong is that they get excited by the bells and whistles and distracted by the shiny lights. They buy technology that looks and sounds exciting, innovative and cutting edge, but they hit one of two problems. Either the technology doesn't work for the way they do business, or they don't really know what they want to achieve with the technology, so those fancy features go unused.

So, what should you do instead? There's no doubt that you should be embracing modern technology in your practice; but innovation should be customer-oriented, not technology driven. What do I mean by this? I mean let your staff and clients drive your technology journey, don't put the technology first. You must find technology that will adapt to your best practice, not the other way around.

When you start to look for technology to use in your practice, it can be easy to get distracted by fancy features. A vendor can demonstrate how a system can automatically collate and page-number your affidavits and annexures, run a conflict check against every single person or entity your firm has ever heard of in less than the time it takes you to say their name, or can apply syntax rules to fields in document templates, but if you don't need any of these things, the system might be no good for you.

The lesson in all of this: you need to really know what you're trying to achieve before you dive in. Understanding your clients' objectives and designing good processes come first. Technology should then be used to enable and enhance your service, not drive it. This will also help with the process of turning your services into products.

Using technology to create powerful customer experiences

Our Probate On The Spot service is delivered by using powerful custom-designed technology that automates much of the process.

We use an interactive 'form' as our file note, and a powerful one at that. Upon clicking 'finish', the form will open the file, prepare the application document and authority, request the disbursement, render the bill and save the form file note. All within seconds.

It now takes me about 15 minutes to prepare an application – but, more than that, it makes for a far better experience for our clients. We can reinvest the time we would have spent on document creation back in the client relationship.

Yes, the technology is the game changer here, but without the process behind it, it would be worthless. The design of the service has become our key competitive advantage. Technology in and of itself is one thing, but how you use it matters more. Technology can easily be copied, but service experiences are much harder to replicate.

What does this mean for you?

There's no doubt that technology can help to improve your business's competitive edge, your customer's experience and, ultimately, your bottom line. More important than any of that, though, technology, along with the other techniques I've spoken about in this book, is the key to freedom. Use technology to automate the grunt work and, ultimately, to help you regain your life.

KEY POINTS IN THIS CHAPTER

1. The people, process, technology golden triangle is missing knowledge as its essential fourth element.

2. Your people are your business's most important asset. In order to find and keep the right people on your team, you need to build a culture that puts people at its heart.

3. Good processes and systems are essential to a business that lets you take a holiday. Invest time in them so you can work hard once.

4. Knowledge management is about leveraging your collective experience by storing, growing and sharing knowledge. You need to make knowledge sharing a way of life in your business.

5. Technology won't replace us, but it will enable you to work faster, better and cheaper. Embrace it, but make sure you customise your technology to suit your unique needs.

 ## IT'S TIME TO DO LAW DIFFERENTLY

- What changes do you need to make so that your people are truly at the heart of your business?

- Identify the essential systems in your business and get started on mapping and improving them.

- Start recording your knowledge by creating simple checklists or file notes that record your most important know-how.

- How can you use technology to eliminate grunt work in your business or to create powerful customer experiences?

Productise and Profit

There we have it, the six steps that will help you reshape your law firm and regain your life.

FIND YOUR VISION | DEEPLY UNDERSTAND YOUR CLIENTS | CREATE AMAZING SOLUTIONS | PRODUCTISE YOUR SERVICES | EMBRACE MODERN MARKETING | OPTIMISE YOUR OPERATIONS

These steps will see you operating your law firm like a true business, one that is built around the work that you love, but whose wheels don't stop spinning simply because you decide to take a holiday.

Profit is about much more than financial gain. The benefits can be broken down into three areas: meaning, money and mastery. These are shown in the table below. You can see the changes you will experience when you reshape your business and develop an ecosystem of legal products.

	Traditional services	Product ecosystem
Money	Time billing Paid in arrears Individual rainmakers	Fixed pricing Paid upfront Business brand
Mastery	Generalist Quality varies Put out fires	Specialist Consistent high quality Managed risk
Meaning	Grunt work Sell knowledge No systems	Work you love Sell solutions Automated systems

Let's briefly consider each of these.

MONEY

More money might not be the driving force for reshaping your firm, but it certainly is a benefit.

First, your profits are no longer a factor of the amount of time you spend working. You charge for your services at fixed prices. Because you're no longer tied to a time sheet, you find efficiencies in the way you deliver work. You've positioned yourself as the expert at what you do, offering a defined solution that is just what your clients need. You can charge a premium.

Products are paid for in advance. When you do your grocery shop, you don't get to the end of each month, work out what you've eaten and then receive a bill for it; you pay before you even take the goods out the shop. Legal products are the same. When you have certainty of price and scope, you can charge in advance by asking your client to pay money into trust. Once the work is completed, you render your bill and pay yourself from trust. Eliminate bad debts forever!

Your law firm is built around a corporate brand, not any one individual rainmaker. Clients come to your firm because of the way you do business. The advantage is that your brand reputation won't leave when an employee does. Untying business success from individual people also makes it easier to scale or sell.

MASTERY

One of the driving forces for many business owners is the sense of self-determination that comes from being in business. Productise and Profit enables you to profit from focusing your work on what you love. By narrowing your businesses focus, eliminating anything that doesn't spark joy and focusing your efforts on providing specific solutions to your client's problems, you become a specialist at what you do. You consistently produce high-quality work and go from putting out fires to more thoughtfully managing risk through your processes and systems.

MEANING

You're no longer selling time or knowledge, but solutions to problems. The products you sell make a real difference to your clients' lives. You've automated your processes and freed yourself from the grunt work, which means you're free to spend your time on the work you love and on the other priorities in life.

KEY POINTS IN THIS CHAPTER

1. By reshaping your firm using my Productise and Profit method, you'll build a product ecosystem that will give you more money, enable you to truly master your craft, and build a more meaningful life.

2. Unlike traditional law, a product ecosystem built following my Productise and Profit method will mean you're paid upfront, fixed prices for the work you do.

3. Delivering specialist products in your product ecosystem will help you and your team become a master at your craft, but the design of your products means that they can be delivered in a way that doesn't depend on you.

4. Not only will Productise and Profit help you to regain your life, it will enable you to do meaningful work you love.

Ready, set, action.
It's up to you to make it happen.

> 'If you really analyze the business landscape, you'll realize that the main difference between mediocre firms and great ones is not just vision, but execution.'

Tim Williams

I hope that by now you're feeling excited and motivated to implement some changes in your business. But I expect that you might also be feeling overwhelmed. Trying to overhaul your business model while also running the business – doing legal work, managing staff, finding new work and everything in between – is no small feat.

How are you going to add the massive task of redesigning your business on top of all you've already got on your plate?

Ideas are easy, implementation less so, but it's only by taking action that you'll create that vision you conjured up at the start of this book. Sooner or later you need to draw a line under the thinking and planning and switch to *doing*.

Most people who read this book already know they want to change their business, they just need the knowledge and a plan to make it happen. This book fills that gap, but even a great plan is no good unless you implement it.

Here's my advice to help you get over those hurdles and take action, once and for all.

TEAMWORK MAKES THE DREAM WORK

I know it's a cliché, but team work really does make the dream work. At Birman & Ride, we take a collaborative approach to all our work, whether it be client files or business development. This collective inspiration and collaborative development is undoubtedly one of the things that contributes to our success. We build on each other's ideas, utilise each other's strengths and help to keep each other motivated. Tackling work as a team means we can keep multiple projects spinning at once and the speed of our development is much faster.

If you have a team, get them involved in project planning and implementation. Choose the projects you enjoy the most to get you started.

If you're a sole practitioner without a team, or need some extra guidance, look for some outside support to help you take your business to the next level.

I started the process to write this book in February 2019. I mapped out the structure and wrote about half of the manuscript, until I gave in to imposter syndrome, uncertainty about style and structure, self-doubt, and dozens of other challenges that, as it turns out, affect almost every author. I knew that if I was going to make it happen then I'd need a guide – someone to help me through the book writing process, coach me through those challenges and to keep me accountable. I joined an author coaching program that gave me the support and accountability I needed, and this time it worked.

Another advantage to having a book coach is that I've undoubtedly ended up with a better book than I would have done without one. Remember back to that cake analogy – why create a process from scratch when you can benefit from the lessons learned by those who have gone before you? It's no different here.

A coach's job isn't to do everything for you; after all, you wouldn't have started your own business if that's what you wanted. Instead, they offer an external vantage point that enables them to see things you can't see. They can help you shift your perspective when you get stuck or pulled off track. They also help keep you accountable. Have you noticed that you're more likely to drag yourself out of bed and get to the gym if you have a workout buddy expecting to see you there? Making a commitment to do a certain thing at a certain time and knowing someone else is expecting you to follow through increases your success in doing so.

Jade Briani Hopper is a retired professional tennis player and now practises as a lawyer. She likens her supervising partner to her tennis coach. Both play an essential role in helping her perform at her best, offering guidance, constructive criticism and support. Professional athletes wouldn't dream of competing in their sport without a coach.[1]

Find a business coach, mentor or accountability group to guide you and see the difference it brings to making change happen.

YOU NEED TO CHANGE THE WAY YOU THINK ABOUT TIME

Aside from uncertainty about what to do next, lack of time is cited as the biggest barrier to implementing change.

The trouble is, if you tell yourself there's not enough time, there probably won't be. You need to change the way you think about time.

Positive psychology has proven that the way we think about things matters. It shows that being optimistic and focusing on positive events

---

1   Jude explains the comparison during our conversation on episode 44 of the Doing Law Differently podcast.

and influences helps people to flourish and live their best lives. Even small shifts in perspective can lead to big shifts in wellbeing and quality of life. By constantly telling yourself that 'there isn't enough time', you're setting yourself up for failure. The starting point needs to be that there is enough time for all the things that are important to you. At the end of the day, there's always enough time for the things you prioritise.

Time management and productivity expert Laura Vanderkam has been a huge influence over the way I perceive time. Vanderkam is the author of several time management books, including *Off the Clock: Feel less busy while getting more done* and *168 Hours: You have more time than you think*. She examines the time logs of thousands of professionals to understand why some busy people feel relaxed about time and others don't. Her theories on using time creatively to achieve goals are much more than the usual hacks we often hear, encouraging us to add up all those tiny snippets of time throughout the day to 'be more productive'.

One of the biggest lessons I've learnt from Vanderkam's work is to think about time in blocks of one week instead of one day. It's really hard to do all the things you want to in one day. If you expect that you'll be able to enjoy a quiet coffee, exercise, read to the kids, get in eight billable hours as well as a good chunk of business development, enough sleep, and meaningful connection with friends or family all in 24 hours, you're setting yourself up to fail.

It's much easier to fit all the things into one week. Divide your week between the competing priorities. Allocate specific times for client work, supervision, business development, phone calls, as well as blank space to allow for those unexpected issues that crop up from time to time. Put first things first – if business development is truly important to you, schedule it for first thing on Monday, not last thing on Friday. And remember Parkinson's law: work expands to fill the time available for its completion.

Are you *really* too busy?

Here's a little exercise. Keep count of each time you say 'I'm too busy' throughout the course of a week. Whether you say it out loud or just think it in your head, make a note of how often you say it and what you're saying it too.

Often 'I'm too busy' is a way of telling someone you don't want to do something – 'I'm too busy doing client work to fix that precedent', or, 'I'm too busy so I'll do this myself instead of teaching someone else how to do it'.

When we say we're too busy, what we really mean is that 'it's not a priority'. See how the perspective shifts when we swap those words.

I've banned myself from saying the words 'I'm too busy'. Instead, when 'I'm too busy' comes into my head as a default response, I force myself to stop and question the truth: is it that this thing isn't a priority to me? If so, then that is my answer: 'The template needs work, but I'm up against a tight deadline with this agreement and I need to get it to the client first.'

Practical tips for time management

Time management is one of my innate skills. I can order and prioritise tasks in my sleep. I know what to do and when to do it to achieve the best effect. I also know that these skills don't come naturally to everyone.

Time management, prioritising and managing expectations are some of the skills I actively set about teaching to junior lawyers. I harp on at them daily about making sure they've kept their task list organised, blocked out time for deep work, and kept on top of all the little tasks that sometimes make us feel like we're drowning.

Once you start thinking about time in a more positive way, the next step is to start implementing some practical strategies to better manage the time you have. Thinking differently is only one piece of the puzzle. To effect change, we also need to act differently.

These are some of the practical strategies that have worked for me and my team.

Block your time

Time blocking involves dividing your day into blocks of time with each block dedicated to a specific task or a specific type of work. Allocate time for innovation and development. You need to schedule it in. It sounds obvious, but it's too easy to let billable work take over. Remember, don't just schedule the idea-building phase, also schedule the 'get it done' phase too.

Focus on the one thing

In his book *The One Thing: The surprisingly simple truth behind extraordinary results*, Gary Keller argues that the key to extraordinary success is focusing each day on the 'one thing' that will make the biggest difference in achieving your goal. Like a domino fall, exceptional success is sequential. You start with the one right thing and focus your energy on it until it topples. Keep doing this and you'll achieve exceptional success.

Keller talks through a sequence of questions to help you determine what your 'one thing' is, ultimately ending up with the focusing question: 'What's the one thing I can do such that by doing it everything else will be easier or unnecessary?'

His point: 'doing the most important thing is always the most important thing'.

Avoid interruptions

If you manage a team, I'll hazard a guess that you feel frustrated with the number of times you're interrupted while trying to get work done – people stopping by to 'just ask a quick question', yet another phone call from that high-maintenance client, or having to drop everything to deal with someone else's error. Many of us spend our entire day in a sea of interruptions, so much so that it gets to 5pm and it feels like we can only truly start our day's work as everyone else starts to leave the office.

Sometimes the interruptions are welcome or necessary, but the sheer volume of them drives you up the wall.

The distraction itself is one thing; the other big issue is the post-distraction period. It takes 23 minutes and 15 seconds to return to the original task and get back up to speed after an interruption.[2]

There's a balance between needing to be available to mentor and support your staff and clients, while at the same time ensuring you have distraction-free time to get through your own work.

So, what can you do? There are the basics, like turning off email notifications, putting your mobile phone on silent, sending your landline to voicemail or closing your office door. A partner at a law firm told me that when she needs distraction-free time, she takes herself off to an empty office on another floor. No one goes looking for her there, so she's able to get her work done interruption-free.

When it comes to managing junior staff, the strategy that has worked the best for me is to have a regular, scheduled meeting with each staff

---

2   'The Cost of Interrupted Work: More Speed and Stress', Gloria Mark. ics.uci.edu/~gmark/chi08-mark.pdf.

member. We use the time to review their files and talk about any other relevant issues. Depending on the staff member's experience, sometimes these meetings will be an hour each day. For more experienced staff, they'll be a few hours a week. I get staff to bring all except urgent issues to me during those dedicated times. In order for this to work, you have to play by your own rules. If a staff member brings you something that isn't urgent, ask them to bring it back during the allocated time. This strategy will take a chunk of time out of your day, but a dedicated block of time is much more effective than constant interruptions.

Surf your personal energy wave

Do you know when you work at your best?

Some people are the most productive first thing in the morning, when their minds are fresh. Some people prefer digging into important work around midday, when their momentum is full throttle, and others leave the most important work for the end of the day when ideas and concepts have had time to settle.

You can cut down on the time it takes you to complete your work by identifying when you work best and planning your most important work for that time. You can boost your productivity even more if you're able to reduce distractions and interruptions during this focused work time.

EXTRAORDINARY GOALS SOMETIMES NEED EXTRAORDINARY PLANS

I'm writing this paragraph at 4:30am on a Sunday morning. For the past few weeks I've dragged myself out of bed at 4am so I can get a decent two-hour chunk of writing in before my children wake up at six. I've written at the hairdressers, on the train to work, in the car while my one-year-old naps, in the garden while the children play on the trampoline and late into the night when I've had a streak going.

When you have extraordinary goals, sometimes you need to achieve them in extraordinary ways.

Perhaps you need to say no to new client work while you take some time to sort your systems and create training materials for new staff. Yes, this will mean a hit to your revenue, but it's short-term pain for long-term gain.

I remember reading about a CEO who worked every day from 5am to 7am on his 'one thing', in his case, certain client work. He'd then go home, have breakfast with his family and drop his children at school, before heading to the office to continue his workday. By time he arrived, he'd already knocked off the most important things he needed to do that day. He was able to engage with his team more effectively, spending his time mentoring, rather than being frustrated and rushing through questions because he needed to get his own work done. An extraordinary effort, but he achieved extraordinary results.

JUST DO THE NEXT RIGHT THING

If you've got young children, or you enjoy a good Disney movie, you'll know where I'm going with this one already. Who'd have thought that a book about legal innovation would take inspiration from Disney's *Frozen*? It just goes to show that inspiration can come from everywhere, not!

With a four-year-old daughter who loves to dance and play pretend and a one-year-old son with a limited vocabulary but who can definitely sing ('oooh oooh oooh oooh, ah ah ah ahhh'), the *Frozen II* soundtrack is on constant repeat in our house.

If you're not familiar with the 'next right thing' story, here's the short version. In the darkest moment of the film, Anna is faced with uncertainty about what to do next after she thinks she has lost her sister Elsa. In the face of grief, sadness and uncertainty, Anna breaks into song (of course) and reminds herself to 'do the next right thing'.

One of the most common questions I'm asked is how to get started with turning ideas into action and implementing change.

The best answer is to just 'do the next right thing'.

As with anything new, change can feel overwhelming and uncertainty about taking the first step often prevents people getting started at all.

Many people are afraid to take the first step. Perhaps the goal seems too far away or the path isn't clear. But taking action is the one thing that separates the leaders from everyone else – they achieved their goals because they stopped thinking and started *doing*.

It doesn't matter if you can't see the path clearly, what matters more is taking the first step.

Remember, you don't need to overhaul your entire business in one swoop. The ideas in this book can be implemented incrementally.

Just do the next right thing.

Change your pricing strategy for one service. Map a process in one area. Ask one customer for feedback. Design one new product. Test one piece of new tech. Experiment with flexible work with one staff member.

What next? Well, I hope you can guess the answer. But just in case, I'll leave you with Anna's wise words:

> *And, with it done, what comes then?*
> *When it's clear that everything will never be the same again*
> *Then I'll make the choice to hear that voice*
> *And do the next right thing.*

KEY POINTS IN THIS CHAPTER

1. Ideas are nothing without execution. It's only by taking action that you'll create that vision you conjured up at the start of this book.

2. Don't try to do it alone. Bring your team on board or get some external guidance to help you bring your vision to life.

3. Change the way you think about time. There's always enough time for the things we prioritise.

4. 'Just do the next right thing.'

Where to from here?

The market for legal services is changing rapidly. Buyers of legal services are no longer willing to accept the way things have always been done, and neither should you.

Failure to adapt will mean your business will be left behind to struggle and fail. But you no longer have to worry about that, because you are holding the solution in your hands. At its heart, the Productise and Profit method is about embracing your role as an entrepreneur and treating your law firm more like a business, so you can finally get out of the trenches and regain your life. When you follow the Productise and Profit method, you'll transform your business from a legal practice dependent on you selling your time to a product ecosystem that is driven by processes and systems and leaves you free to do the work you love, and also to get more time out of the business to enjoy as well.

This book puts those pieces together into a six-step blueprint you can implement in your firm to transform your business. The six steps to Productise and Profit are:

1. **Find your vision:** if you're going to reshape your business, you might as well make it one you love. You can redesign your business to suit your life.

2. **Deeply understand your clients:** use your client's needs, desires and frustrations as your starting point and you'll end with innovative solutions that solve their problems.

3. **Create amazing solutions:** your clients don't care about how much time something takes you, they want solutions to their problems, and those problems are often bigger than legal issues.

4. **Productise your services:** make it easier to attract, convert and deliver by turning your services into products with a predefined scope, a fixed price and a system or method for delivery. Build a product ecosystem that delivers outstanding value but isn't dependent on you.

5. **Embrace modern marketing:** draw potential clients in by educating them and shedding light onto their problem and your solution through quality content.

6. **Optimise your operations:** improve the behind-the-scenes of your business operations through a focus on people, process, knowledge management and technology.

The great news is that you have an opportunity to reshape your business; to build the business you want and deserve, not the business you think others expect of you or that has been forced on you by circumstances. I know this seems daunting, but now you have a system to follow.

And remember, what do you do when you're overwhelmed and don't know where to turn?

Just do the next right thing.

Not tomorrow. Today. Right now.

It's time to do law differently.

Looking for an engaging speaker for your live or virtual event?

Lucy Dickens is an experienced speaker and facilitator who inspires new ways of thinking and motivates people into action. Her presentations are full of stories and practical tips and delivered with passion.

Lucy loves to speak about law firm transformation, legal practice management and operations and the career/family juggle.

> 'Lucy is an energetic facilitator with great presence. She engaged a room of 30 lawyers, across different practice areas and a big age range – she had the room buzzing, which was impressive. Her presentation was very well structured and her material was beautifully presented. She is very authentic in her delivery and was lovely to deal with before and after her session. I would highly recommend her for facilitation or speaking engagements.'

Carmen Maughan, Senior Professional Development Officer,
The Law Society of Western Australia

If you're interested in getting Lucy to speak at your next event, either face to face or virtually, email **lucy@lucydickens.com.au**.

www.lucydickens.com.au

Doing Law Differently podcast

Join Lucy Join Lucy Dickens in her weekly conversations with forward-thinking leaders in law who share how they're doing law differently.

There's lots of talk about why we need to change the legal industry, but much less about how to do it. The Doing Law Differently podcast takes a practical look at the behind-the-scenes of progressive law companies which are reinventing legal practice and transforming the profession for the better. Lucy interviews leaders in the profession who are walking the talk of NewLaw and who are willing to share not just what they're doing differently, but how they're doing it.

From alternative fee arrangements and new technology to innovative business models and new ways of delivering services, we find out what NewLaw looks like from the inside.

> 'I am loving hearing the real, practical, nitty gritty of exactly how law firms are doing law differently as I try to build my own "different" practice.'

> 'I always feel inspired after listening, Lucy! Thank you for spending time to make this awesome podcast!'

Find the show at **www.doinglawdifferently.com.au**, on Google Podcasts, Apple Podcasts, Spotify or your favourite podcast app or connect with Lucy on LinkedIn to hear about the latest episodes (www.linkedin.com/in/lucy-dickens).

www.lucydickens.com.au

Need some one-to-one guidance with your law firm transformation?

Each year Lucy works with a handful of clients one on one over a period of 3, 6 or 12 months to help them transform their law firm.

Her role is to help you design a vision for your business that aligns with your goals for your life and then to give you the strategies, guidance, support and accountability you need to take your vision from idea to reality. Lucy will provide the mentorship, training and accountability you need to help you achieve your goals.

The one message you will have taken away from this book is that nothing changes without action. Along with training and mentoring, Lucy provides accountability, objective feedback and an expectation for progress. She wants you to implement change, not just come up with ideas.

'Lucy is an amazing business coach. I have so many ideas and dreams for my ideal business, but I was really struggling to implement them on my own. I am so glad I reached out to Lucy; she is a one of a kind she is genuine and caring and I feel she is really invested in the process. She also takes an innovative and in-depth approach to creating a business that really matters to me and how I can best serve my clients.'

Josephine Cockerill, Lawyer

If you'd like to find out more about working with Lucy, please email **lucy@lucydickens. com.au.**

www.lucydickens.com.au

Reshape your firm and regain your life

Prepare to Productise & Profit!

If you loved this book, why not sign up for Lucy's new program, Productise & Profit!

This is a three-month program designed to help law firm leaders on their journey to reshape their firm and regain their life.

Lucy's program offers practical support and guidance to help you implement the Productise & Profit method in your business.

Lucy will not only coach (help you find the right answers), she'll also mentor (show you the best way) and teach (show you how to do it).

> 'Lucy's coaching has been a gamechanger for me and my business. Not only is her experience and insight invaluable but her personalised approach is refreshing. She doesn't try to make me or my business fit a rigid mould. Rather, she looks at the bigger picture and provides practical guidance on how I can achieve my personal goals for business, law and life. She helps turn business ideas into reality.'
>
> **Nikolina Palasrinne,** Founder and Principal, Rubix Legal

If you'd like to know more about doing Lucy's program either individually or as part of a group, **email lucy@lucydickens.com.au.**

www.lucydickens.com.au

Would you like to interview Lucy Dickens?

Lucy can talk with passion and authority about:

- The transformation of law firm business models

- Productising legal services

- Law firm practice management

- Training and mentoring junior legal practitioners

- The career/family juggle

If you would like to interview Lucy about any of the above, or her latest book *It's Time to Do Law Differently: How to reshape your firm and reclaim your life*, please email **lucy@lucydickens.com.au**.

CPSIA information can be obtained
at www.ICGtesting.com
Printed in the USA
LVHW051102241120
672558LV00003B/252

9 781922 391612